CLOSER TO THE HOUR

Red Jordan
Arobateau

Closer To The Hour

Journal #24 in the Journey Series

Any resemblance to any person living or dead is purely coincidental.

All un-attributed quotes are from the Prophet Red Jordan Arobateau.

ISBN: 978-1-304-85387-5

Published by RED JORDAN PRESS
Redjordanarobateau.com
USA

Part- 1

I think we have always been brave—even 60 million years ago, the monkey tribes, learning to walk upright in order to see over the tops of tall grasses watching for predators; assembling their tribe to keep moving towards abundant food, water; facing death everywhere— assault from savage beasts, dehydration from lack of water, no food supply—& starvation; having to find shelter in caves, trees. So brave!

These are the days of comparative freedom—as said, am not yet harnessed up to the yoke; or rather am harnessed to the yoke of a different sort—have not yet been Called Up. To make Allelia, as it is said in the Hebrew (which Christianity is from) make Allelia --

Friday, December 20
FUN @ Coyote.

Am @ Infernal One PU art file to show galleries.

I will know where I am placed.

Bright sun @ Hos.

Saw Gary & Rich:

> Your boyfriend was here.
>
> Yeah?
>
> Told him you'd be back @ 3.

Needless to say am saving $ by not seeing Him! Gary gave him $2; he got a box of sugar cookies and left us 2 of them which I ate 1.5 & set the other half on a garbage can for homeless.

Saw the bird w/tied foot. Fed it, it is very tame. Called Annie and told her the situation. Need someone to grab/hold bird while I cut the wire. Or visa-versa. Scissors in backpack.

Somebody scared bird away. —Waited w/crumbs in hand for bird to reappear—but didn't see it. Relaxing, my hand opened, crumbs fell—

4

to the sidewalk; immediately the whirr of wings, bird swooped down; dined, then was scared off again.

The OM sat in the declining sun.

God thank You for getting me here this far—another Christmas, Felitiz Navidad.

Everybody has a time.

OM was arrived w/his NOTES in his pocket.

Assembling this Gallery File remember my Grant Writing efforts. Reading the requirements, assemble materials, getting technical help to create files, wrapping, mailing, all requires an investment of $, of time; if you are declined over time after time of making fruitless efforts you may be defeated.

Well, am trying a new approach by hitting up the Gallery's in New Year. Making a short list of them.

The OM sat outside on one of his ledges @ Sushi Rika—he gazed across street @ stoplight to test his eye. He could not see the red color—stop. Nor discern when it changed to green. Could discern shapes, objects, people, vehicles, —but not very well. Dr had stated: *I see by the tests the inflammation is reduced.*

> They are being rude in a pushy way a really subtle way. That shows the mentality of this society.
> --A Ho

We discuss a transsexual friend, Asian, who found to his dismay:

> Now that I'm male I get more encouragement, more approval from my family, from my mom, my dad my sisters.

They like him more now that he's a man and it makes him mad.

> You must remember, we are spiritual beings having a physical experience.
> --A Ho

5

> But what is love: --if it is divided, limited, put into directions and you are told you must go no other way but theirs. It deviates. The WHOLE, that is love. Love must contain everything & everybody. Then, this woman was also an outsider. Looking at me as if I were the STRANGER.
> --STRANGE EMBRACE OF A PRODIGAL

Fell into bed, slept until 4 am; now up to take shower and go to bed.

I think of young sea turtles riding the 7-seas.

Actually the religious education am getting @ Grace is the best in the world—spiritual & in intellect.

Scriptures are a text to be read, inspired, examined; taught.

Love. Loved by intelligence. Higher, greater, unfathomable; tempered by love. Love, instructed by intelligence.

To make all—even the lost— realize they are part of the human family.

Saturday, December 21; Winter Solstice!
Walked to Coyote, spoke w/St Joan, she elated, keeping self-positive great mood during this emotion-loaded season. Has cut off invitations from her toxic relatives. Was soon joined by Olde Jolly:

> Have you ever done 2 blowjobs @ the same time?
>
> You have!
>
> Yes!

Left after the sun disappeared; Ho's, joined by the Grace contingent— Denis, The Malaysian, and soon Annie appeared, unexpectedly, on her way pajama-shopping.

Had enjoyed brief minutes of sun.

6

Gave sweets in bag found in front of my apartment to the 2, then left the bag's remainder in homeless man's doorway.

PM
Am waiting for A Ho to return from Macys to PU me and off to din! She has to buy winter PJ's for grandmother's companion.

@ the end what does any of this matter? What does it mean— literally nothing! How you dress, how much $ you have.

In Scheziuan restaurant—OM had a dish he'd never tasted before, found it quite favorable. Being from Scheziuan Province it is not on ordinary Chinese menus. He watched huge TV screen w/Asian entertainers, young lithe bodies. Affluence was the backdrop for this video—most of the world's people do not live in such riches—this is the upper 5%. Lavish surroundings, svelte young Asian model in a gown, her escort in a tux, a sumptuous feast table, silver & gold, satins & silks. Jewelry; *bling.*

After dining they stopped to view the store, in which is an aquarium. He saw all the fish, smooth silver, scales, fins, eyes set, black; big mouths; up turned faces; so many souls in this aquarium thousands of fishes, so much life!

Annie Ho is living on a precipice currently, at the intersection of her grandmother's impending demise, & awaiting her status from the INS immigration service. What will come first? Can her grandmother buy her into an American business? Can she get her student visa back? Multimillions of decent people are living thru this in America awaiting all this immigration snafu to be un-gnarled.

Sunday, December 22, 2PM
Slept all last nite, and most of today.

These birds are so loud, so noisy, but they never were like that! When they were cage mates—their soft warm bodies pressed together @ nite assured each other! Now they are hell! Squawking squawking—because they want something! When they were coupled they wanted for nothing! They had food, water, outings in flight, each other!

7

Dusted off excellent picture frames scored from the old Trans Center—and put them up on the painting rack out of the way as to clear out space beside new book storage plastic boxes shelves—per instructions from On High.

Annie & I have been dining around town—which for her is a food-binge program. She won't eat for 3 days, then we dine @ 4 establishments in a row!

> Taiwanese restaurant
> 24-hour donut shop
> My Place Chinese café
> 24-hour donut shop again!

I take out food from each place, but today, Sunday, have the feeling of being full. Have had to throw out portions of each Meal trey—sweet fruit, potatoes or rice, breaded part of meat, or noodles, which constitute a bed under the meat. All starch/carbohydrates. Will get it right. Am eating more vegetables then ever before In The Life!

After meditation, he had a mind-vision that the good Lord in all tenderness had bent down & cleaned out huge amount of yellow earwax out of his ear so he could really hear.

On wei to church.

Laundress woman washing in Laundromat 7th day of the week, until she wears out.

Festive. Everything is ever-green; sno-white & Santa red.

Our church is making $—see the Christmas concert is Sold Out.

OM had been tapping around w/his cane so he had familiarity w/every square inch of the cathedral. He went here & there. Now he waited for service to begin, outdoors. The constant stomping, pacing energy of children behind him on the labyrinth.

Out on the plaza. Fountain gushes bright red, orange, lime green, —
white light, spouts.

So this is it. Last Sunday before Christmas. Jampacked organ
concert. Birth of Christ, stirring of faith. The Cross hung—full
bodied. Meaty human flesh twisting in agony, dying under its own
weight.

OM exhausted had slept all day—had he indulged in 2 much sugar?
Had he worn himself down thru his perpetual schedule? Was it is T-
shot coming up soon—but not for 3 more days?

Verged on feeling bad. He wanted for something he did not have.
Was lagging, without his usual energy to pep him up into a positive
mood. His NOTES sheaf fell *splat*—on the white marble floor of the
cathedral. To PU them up was an effort. Even to put pen to paper a
chore.

So this was a snobby church—& he had no close friends here—but
Annie was his friend.

Repair. Said the Lord.

You can do amazing good w/your gifts; says the Lord(ess).

Thought he'd share his food basket w/Junior if the lad ever showed
up.

Music trilled like a brook from the pianist; our Priests, lambs, dressed
in white robes, prepared to take their seats.

Purifying our conscious thru your constant instruction, oh God.

Repair.

Christ was a Scandal! From his beginning, to his demise. The
pregnancy of Jesus to an unwed woman was shame. Scorn—he died
on the Cross. To die on a cross was an object of scorn in 30 BC. It
was a punishment used to deter thieves, criminals; social dissidents.
Excellent sermon courtesy of Priest Jude Harmon.

9

Me & Annie went to the gritty Pakistani-Indian restaurant in TL, full of Indians, a few women in beautiful Indian wear— hijab/sari fashion.

We noticed a bullet hole thru the restaurant's front plate glass window, a spider web out in circles around it.

Skeleton size crackheads pick thru the streets outside, locked forever inside their brain.

Next we are patrons in the My Place Chinese café.

Went w/Annie to eat 3 deserts—and myself 3 scrambled eggs w/cheese…

Patrons in here gaze @ TV w/no recognition of what is going on— there is nothing but shit on TV.

As we made our way home, driving smoothly in grandmother-bought new car. The moon was a 3/4ths, the other ¼ having been eaten away; brown red, a fleshy color. The moon looked like it was ready to drop to the ground.

PM
Nada.

Monday, December 23
I know I am typecasted and race cast. I know I am a stranger. People view my friends in one way—me in another, not so good.

On street saw the blax accordion player, he has turned 56—

> Thought I'd have to give up my room, but a lady friend she gave me $500—to get my accordion. I can't get Meals On Wheels, I'm not a senior. 4-more years to go. I'd rather to earn my money playing my accordion. I can keep my room.

He had to keep turning the wheel of his work—no matter if he was a bit blue:

Jasmin peevish @ him for mentioning the 3 sacks of laundry he
wanted her to do— for her In Home Health Service. No Junior seen

I must say God did keep me out of trouble. —By giving me a job
made me think I had power, great power to make a dent in the
world—being an artist/writer; & only now approaching age 70 do
things come clear—I might not be that great a prophet; but he had a
life—a purpose, & still do. — I must finish.

Off w/Annie Ho again to dine!

This is a world-class city you are going to have friends of all
nationalities, colors, dialects.

Man recognize from building; speaks Rooski lingo—he offered me an
attaché case he was throwing out, saying—*I just got a new one.* As I
exited building saw 2 girls headed towards the man—all spoke in
Russian accents, and one was blond! Aurrrgh! Was it the blond
Rooski I had battled w/on the steps 6 months ago who would not
budge off the steps to let me & my laundry go past, and so I
complained repeatedly to the building manager and to the downtown
manager! & here he, their friend, had been friendly and done me a
kindness!

Table is always sticky @ Pakistani restaurant. Indian music,
women's voice singing Hindi over the sound system. Windows
steamed. Comfortable, working class. There is street memorial right
down the block descending, where someone died—by murder.
Gunned down right there in the public street; his last living breath
taken there beside a gritty brick tenement. A religious candle;
sympathy cards, public writings of folks who knew the man; in a
shrine built against the wall—6 empty beer bottles sat there too—
symbolizing the passed man's pastime. Rest in Peace.

The lavatory @ Pakistani restaurant is dungeon like—dangerous stairs
descend turning twice; they are covered in sheet of rubber which has
come loose buckled and is slipping off each stair! W/holes in it!
HAR! Sticky stair rails to hold onto, thankfully. The toilet will not
digest a paper towel some careless person has thrown into it.

Annie is truly in a horrible situation—set up inadvertently by people acting on her behalf, and her, society-shy, naive, and young, —an obedient Chinese Granddaughter allowing this to go on w/out stepping in to speak up for herself.

I am going from 1 Hong Kong hell to another—except this one's in America!

Annie hollering & screaming horribly in car about her awful predicament, her grandmother, her mother in Hong Kong who really did abuse her, her great frustration not knowing what immigration is going to do to her—and not having taken control of her own personal situation because she's never been taught how to take charge of her own life decisions! –To stand up for herself!

PM

They do this to frighten you—their hate. Letters from Medical. From Foodstamps. Now in the week between letter #1, which said I would get $187 per month, (from $88) to letter #2 which now says I will get only $90 per month, (which has been changed from $88...)

The church has always been too conservative, timid, siding w/dictators to secure its own survival.

> The Muslim Brotherhood has shown its ugly face as a terrorist organization.
> --French TV

It was a crude bomb; a keg of nails/set in a canister filled w/explosives; kills 14 @ police station.

I always thought this was so. That Brotherhood. Thought they'd smoothly shove their man into place after the Egyptian freedom riots. After all those Egyptian women & men rioted in the streets for their freedom! For a Democracy!

Now they've been stripped of power.

And here is this Muslim brotherhood sitting up here on the throne as pretty as you please! —How about equal rights for non-believers? Where did this come from? This is not freedom! It is not democracy!

Oh, must mention in reading over NOTES concerning Coyote, me & @ least several other persons silently feel the rabid Owner will have poisoned the new owners minds, talking trash about us! May have given a list of *people to watch out for!* Many of us are sure we are on that list!

Go to sleep click off TV; w/billowing smoke on the screen, Syria in flames.

Tuesday, December 24, Christmas Eve!
Well the toxic presence of the Owner is vanishing…

Sun shines bright @ Coyote.

Tables & chairs set out on every square inch of the frontage including parklet.

Christmas music plays. Café will stay open until 7 pm.

The particular little hell is over.

When sun is out it is hot, minute the flaming orb dips over the roofs— cold sets in.

Left Coyote after brief sojourn w/Rich & Singing Man; things have changed there. @ Hos sun is full bright hot as it not yet dipped away over the roofs.

Wait for the Malaysian.

Tomorrow is the big day—the big loaded day. Christ's birthday; cause of suicide; angst ridden; family turmoil; calendar marks Dec 25 as the heaviest-duty emotional holiday of the year.

Some sit there waiting to die. I'm waiting to live.

Saw sleeping homeless on sidewalk—same size & shape of Junior. Lay covered w/blankets; peeked around looked @ his face— wrinkled, grizzly. Would I still like Junior when he looks like that?

PM
Dock-*que*-ments.

> *Your destiny calls*
> *Thru an open*
> *barroom door.*

Oh, early AM saw Sister Wendy in her convent—The Order of the Carmelite Nuns. Sister has a spot there as a hermit—living in a caravan (trailer) in isolation, in their woods. She comes in to prayer; does not sit down in the chapel w/the other nuns, but up in the belfry, alone.

Wednesday, December 25, Christmas Day!
Sky-bleu car appears; Jasmin PU me.

Sister Wendy spoke of today's society:

> So much noise, distraction. There is never peace for reflectivness. For contemplation. People are trained to be entertained non-stop.

So when Jasmin & me stopped for gas, it was a newly purchased station doing their best to win customers; they had a loudspeaker out by the pumps which blared out a non-stop dialogue of advertisements: *come & get your soft drinks right here in our store, remember while your pumping gas, shop in our store right now!*

You think you'd get a moments peace seated in car waiting for the gasoline to pump.

Jasmin had on an oldies station on car radio:

> I remember dancing to all these tunes. In the 1970's on the dance floor—before that, in the 1960's dancing around the jukebox on red/black carpet in queer bars which allowed no dancing in couples, but if a mad fool danced alone, popping fingers, stomping feet,

shaking butt; in their lonely world, nobody could say much about that.

7-dogs race around Dalora's house!

4 of the dogs leaping into my lap excitedly! Leap in, then off, and spin madly around the room!

Very nice, holistic afternoon @ Delora's. She did one bag of laundry for me. The other 2 remain there, for her to bring @ her convenience—part of her new work.

Delicious dinner w/turkey & ham; greens, biscuits. YUM!

And COFFEE!

Watched some mad stuff on the telly.

Watched dogs almost as much!

PM
It is really bad to discriminate against a person—unfairly—they take it to heart—lower self-esteem; they begin to act this out in negative ways.

Frankly he was thinking about the toxic owner's judgment of him. Refusing to let him use the restroom! His rights as a citizen!

Thursday, December 26
You are not going to spend money in a place where you can't go to the bathroom. So TM, like others brought their own coffee! Sad state of affairs for a coffee shop. –In business to make money!

Others would get up from table and declare: *I'll be back, I'm going to buy a coffee—I'll be back in 20 minutes.* Needless to say they weren't going directly into the café door to buy it, but down the block & round the corner to Van Ness to Starfucks to buy that coffee. Quite a few customers had begun to do this and came back and sat up there on the Owners cheap wretched chairs being non-customers.

The transsexual position in the gay world, in life itself, is very uncertain.

Be decent—that's all I ask. Say's the Lord(ess).

The day @ Coyote was brief. He arrived to see 3 OGM's w/a place for him to sit. First words out were:

> He's gone.
>
> Is he really gone?
>
> No more. He's really gone.

Just then one of the waitresses the Owner had tortured appeared and she verified w/a smile that he was indeed gone: *Yes he's gone! Truly gone.*

Immediately TM dashed in & purchased himself a medium-size coffee. It was his first direct purchase in the joint for 3 months!

I'm back! As a purchasing customer!

He called Jasmin to remind her of his wake-up call the next AM:

> 8-dogs!
>
> That's right!
>
> Yow!

I've got 8 dogs here! She spoke, brightly.

PM
Well it turned out very well. Maybe it was the prayer!

People are always doing something stupid:

> Man rescued from the back of a garbage truck—how did he get stuck in the back of a garbage truck in the first place?

16

Dogs, horses, cows, cats, are forever being rescued from walls, wells, cliffs, oceans, rooftops, crevices, boards floating in a flood. Animals rescued w/chagrined looks on their faces—bears heads stuck inside tree holes, etcetera.

This just shows you how stupid the human/animal genome is. But we are loved! Remember, despite it all!

> If you are Richard Sera (Sculptor)—are you competing against yourself?
> --Charlie Rose to sculptor Richard Sera; TV

In the 1940's, researchers won Nobel Prize for their study on bees that do the wobble dance. The wobble dance signals to the other bees a new direction to get to somewhere important.

The bee flies back to the hive w/news of its tremendous discovery— an unheard of source of pollen, or a perfect spot for a new hive. The bee lands among its fellow bees and begins a circular dance, legs moving, wings buzzing, going round and round, but at one point in every turn it begins to shake its tail and wobble visibly, this point in the turn indicates a direction! It might be miles away, but if the other bees follow that direction they will discover what the bee has found! The group of bees who have witnessed the wobble dance take off w/the bee and buzz back to the new site; examine it, and, satisfied, all of them return to the hive—where all who have now witnessed the find proceed to do the wobble dance. Fairly soon the entire hive has been shown the new direction—and @ once the entire hive takes off to their new home.

Bees this way speak w/out words.

The Holy Spirit talks to me sometimes thru indication, thru visual presentation, & not thru words.

Friday, December 27, (Shabbat)
Photo of a spaceship blasting off earth—*that is the answer*. The OM thought. He was in the waiting room of the clinic, waiting for his blood draw.

17

Most hideous & horrifying news @ clinic—my appointments, prescriptions have lagged, dragged all these years because of: *Red, we have you listed twice in our system—under 2 different medical record numbers!*

One Male, one Female! AUUURRRRRR RRRUUUGHHHH!

Saw soul bro-sis; dark black skin, w/large dreads @ Castro clinic. He is cleaned up alcohol, carries a bedroll and newly homeless. He speaks of going back to De-troit. His art will flourish back there w/out the constant draining high-rent situation haunting him here in this hi-assed price global greed city.

No sun today, rain in the air, which probably won't happen. Life is hard. Mellow music soothes. Piped from out the Café speakers. Spoke w/these 2 younger TG souls; one MTF, the other FTM— maybe. Both are housing challenged.

@ the Ho's, man goes up to coffee pot, fills a gigantic Starfucks coffee cup w/coffee—draining the small canister. That cup would hold 8 or 10 of the small taster cups put out for the shoppers! How selfish! He is the 2nd person I've seen do this cute trick—both Chinee—Whoops! Well now to call one of my Chinese friends, hopefully to go funning…

Saw Grace people—the Cathedral has put out a call out for a new Presenter—a priest—one who can *sing!* Ha Ha Ha!!!!!

It is quite difficult for some of these non-musically trained priests to sing their way thru the prayers—yet this is what the Cathedral calls for, its scriptural I guess, or traditional.

Seated on a ledge, resting, as he walked home, the OM observed that all the dogs in this town of SF wear clothes; nice, colorful, expensive dog coats & see their little tails wagging under them, feet stepping fast they keep pace w/their long-legged human companions.

Laundromat; white man comes in sticks bills in coin change machine, receives handfuls of silver quarters—this is suppose to be for us doing our laundry—not any fool off the street; you won't get mad @ this until the machine runs out of change and it is your clothes that are wet! If there is free stuff everybody will steal it rich & poor person alike!

Surprise you don't see rich people out in line @ St Anthony food kitchen!

In the Laundromat saw mo' problems; not enough baskets to carry wet clothes from washer to dryer. People hoard these baskets, spend leisure time taking out one pr socks @ a time carefully folding them.

T stood outside the Laundromat in the street in the cold, waiting for his clothes to dry. He saw the ancient wrought iron fence 10 feet across which enclosed a small stretch of woodsy yard between tenement buildings, a hold-over from yesteryear, and prayed for the possum he'd once saw lumbering over the 6-foot tall fence; a wild creature in downtown SF back yards trying to make its home and forage in such a small space amid such danger.

That the pain might lift; that they might all have homes.

The OM went back inside his familiar studio. The Spirit put words in his mouth:

> *Come back to my home.*

> Come back to my home? I have a home up there? Huh.

> *A fine home, room for all. All comforts. All animals, people. Life.*

That horrid hateful Laundromat—my stuff came out of its dryer cool, air-dried, instead of hot; some clothes still damp, must be hung up!

PM
Birds out; first time in 2 weeks. They sit, grooming each other on my shoulders. Am still resting from the long strain of Penny Cat's illness, dust mite stress, Medical insurance snafu, & money-catching up.

Repulsive TV item about whipping women publicly in Sudan, Africa, for Islamic violation of harsh Shari law. In this case a woman riding in a car w/a man who is not her relative. —Public disorder. A strong black woman's rights advocate spoke how women's organizations are fighting these backward laws.

See woman dressed in traditional robes, head scarf squatting on ground two male police officers stand, each holds a bull whip, one lashes her, then the other, w/his bullwhip. A crowd of women in robes & headscarves and a few men watch on.

What a disgusting sight.

One can see why many white Europeans & Americans began to drift away from religion 2 generations ago, in the early 1900rds. —Because of similar, tho not as draconian laws—laws which ruin people's lives. –All for the sake of some Pope or preacher and his bible-interpretations.

Case in point, as mentioned my dad could not marry his girlfriend because she was a Catholic, and their ruling was a Catholic could not marry a divorced person.

Many of these people @ Grace are professional, well educated, had good jobs, and good retirement; you won't see them down in the food line @ Glide memorial church w/a ticket in their hand waiting for a 2nd plate, I'll tell you!

PBS TV spoke of growing dissatisfaction of some SF residents vs., the greedy money-affluent new tekkies sprung up like weeds in San Jose Silicon Valley driving us poor out of our homes, out of our communities. It mentioned the bus blocking protests—in which the giant obnoxious corporate busses that transport wealthy tekkies to their jobs are blocked by protesters.

Maybe the ignorant tekkies will look out of their tinted glass windows and see reality out there carrying their picket signs & howling @ them to: **go home yuppie!**

More on TV about Golden Dawn, the fascist Neo-Nazi murderous Greek political organization—which is the 3rd strongest political party in that nation. They are a backlash against the unresolved issues w/immigrants—as are many European countries.

Oh did I tell you the file of my Art File to Show Galleries is done—but the disc copy cost $10. I can't afford to leave the disc w/galleries—and couldn't afford to purchase but one. Also it's on my flashdrive.

When he Crossed himself that nite he felt all these times he'd repeated that motion he'd been slowly opening up his heart, his heart charka was opening up, pure, to radiate the truth, & to absorb the truth, to be pure, light of the Eternal dwelling in there, his heart, opening up to feel emotions for all the people, animals of the world.

Maybe magic would flow out of it! Maybe healing—this is what Christ had been talking about!

Saturday, December 28
OM felt himself out the door w/his cane.

Studio. $1,850.

When young yuppies complain about SF high assed prices—what do you think its doing to us who been living her 30, 40-years? A lifetime?

There is a new For Sale sign on Bush Street apartment building; realtor Indian surname.

Did I mention the Malaysian's building is up for sale—again—for the 4th time changing hands—flipping for millions profit.

Each flip makes this older woman nervous & more nervous.

Kaplan's—the Army/Navy store where OM as a youth in his 20's purchased work clothes —is selling their property. Kaplan's will be no more. A fantastic amount of cash exchanged hands—because of Twitter Internet buying the old Merchandise Mart building nearby; this is kapitalism gone amuck along the Market Street corridor— Kaplan's selling for a gigantic profit—where as they might have stayed for another generation, to provide their togs for the ranks of us outlaws, artists, activists.

@ Coyote w/OGM—now Hos—saw homeless Pakistani's on bench across from me; grungy shabby clothes, sandals, blankets rolled up. There is a whole new wave of underclass & homeless Pakistani's who are dropping out of their dirt-poor parents social network into the streets.

An employee took his break; brushed his luxuriant beard on a Hos shopping bench.

@ Miz Daisy's apartment building lobby; site of the first station of her Birthday Party; just setting up—a lot of liquor is flowing. After cruising men on Polk Street—here, in this very straight place have to check my glance @ the door!

Cannot let my eyes drift lower then neck level! Don't dare let my gaze linger on any men's nuts!

These are chiefly hard-working union employees. Women, men. Some higher positions in the union.

Everyone drinks from paper cups. Someone goes to open a wine bottle. The Brandy canister is popular. This is the beginning of the party—before the food.

Looking about for a corkscrew—the old one dangles, broken, outside a wine bottle. They await the arrival of a delivery.

We just started drinken'.

Set a heavy packages on table—full of wine bottles, brandy, whisky. Soon table held 16- multi color bottles.

We follow an accustomed rouine.

Now we walk down the street to the sushi restaurant.

Somebody toasts Miz Daisy, saying—*Daisy came here & got into our hearts.*

Holidays still are not over—there's still New Years. Biz closed. People gone.

Another beautiful birthday party, Miz Daisy—Japanese food. Then Annie & I take off for Clement Street.

We are now in My Favorite Place, Chinese.

I hope my work benefits humanity. I hope I have earned my keep.

PM
History of the world has been one of motion; ancient ancestors following animal herds; the herds have been in motion since before humans ever appeared on the landscape, following seasonal grazing.

People who have a spirituality have better lives because they have a companion—something w/them upon their journey from their first pains to death; this companion is w/all of us but if you don't *have* it—*know it* —it is like walking a journey w/a lead shield between you & the companion so that you can't feel, nor have faith, nor see, or know & you think you are alone. And how lonely & miserable that can be!

I would like to think one day my voice will get out; all people will see my JOURNEY journals.

I was young; eyes full of wonder, I expected I was going to go out to conquer the world.

Sunday, December 29
I'm going to see my father again.

Christmas is past. New Years is here.

Mounting steps up the long hill to Grace. Now @ the Great Stairs. Tourists cameras snap, film whirs.

Tourists. --Scum on the real life of SF.

Musicians for the evening's service were practicing Alleluias. A Ho holds a pitcher of water; is watering the red leaf Poinsettias.

He noticed when he came in people who knew him and he knew them would look away and talk among themselves. Not greeting him but one day when he was in his success they would! (Turn to him w/eager faces.) How hypocritical.

T-Man saw a smallish man in an elegant suit, well groomed & not *fat*. He turned up his nose; he turned to light his candle: *you approach Me w/hate in your heart?* He immediately agreed, bowing and tossed the vision of the smallish man into his trash basket of hate, wiping it clean.

The staff scurried around the cathedral choir loft doing various tasks; —their feet scuffle w/echoes over the marble floor. Set up podium, communion tables; human-size candles. Icons and votive candles— the little blue lights. Tinkling piano.

Final touch Elaine, Verger, set down upon the table the magnificent silver-bound bible; he saw how everything was glittery.

He bowed his head, leaning over the Holy Water font, dips his fingers down, down, into the alabaster basin—but it was dry! The Spirit said to him: *The Father will see you tonight.*

Saw this @ the font. So the Father (scriptural interpretation) was going to come to him tonight; last nite in the choir loft, last nite of Advent, which had arrived!

—T did not mind the wild wind, which swept the plaza he was use to being out in the cold, alone. On wei to toilets there.

The plaza is restored; all heavy-duty machinery removed, the job is over; grand, the plaza stretches out full, pristine.

Where a human exercises its merry dog; wind blows; trees are lit up like Christmas across in Huntington Park; glow bright; yuletide trees green & red; boughs uplifted like Hanukah menorahs.

6-bongs of the chimes in belfry tower.

The service begins.

Angles & archangels. Cherubim and seraphim.

Lovely harp; blax sister plucked the strings of the ancient angelic instrument.

There were too many blue blazing votive candles to count.

Hands grasped each other during the Passing Of The Peace. He gripped a white warm hand; in a long handshake; milked its fingers like a cows teats for human closeness.

Thank You God for always giving me friends—he remembered NYC; age 16, met Queer Jewish girls from Brooklyn in Greenwich Village by the fountain under the Arc de Triumph. Hyde Park, Chicago, blax artists @ the Promontory, —by the water; poets, writers, artists, & musicians. Now am here on Polk Strassa w/OGM's, a band of them.

W/out God what a torturous existence this would be—without a way out; without a Creator, a Christ, a Prophet, to believe in; my purpose, *to follow You.*

The OM sat in the front row of the congregation @ the 6—which was held in the great quire loft for Advent season; he looked @ the gothic wall before him, up some 4 stories high where marble statues hung in space:

Like the prophets who were before you.

That busy little creature scurrying around ushering, handing church leaflets out to the arriving congregants. As it gets closer to the hour of her deportation, pray she might not have to go. –Off to a foreign land 7,000 miles away.

Primitive peoples huddled by the campfire, if an advanced civilization was to hand them a plate of food—they would eat off of it. Once the advanced civilized people left, it would be logical to think the primitives would go to the empty plate and wait, staring @ it, expecting food would appear on this plate—simply not understanding the dynamics of it all, never having seen a plate before. –How someone must prepare this food, and place it on the plate. And I'm thinking maybe what we ask for from God can be something like this dynamic, there is some connecting action missing that we are not aware of, that we must discover.

We pray for some answer—

> Christ is the child of God—by lineage.
> Buddha did not say he was God, but a seeker of the Great Rules of life.
> Mohammad said he was a Prophet of God.
> --From the service

In helping a person, speaking to them, being their friend, you must cut thru their shit w/a hacksaw—a chain saw; a sledge hammer breaking apart the thick concrete of all the old layers of everything—what they've been taught, what they've suffered:

> Church school when I was so young before we are able to think they tell us this is wrong, that is wrong.

XX is a mess of energy. We went to Sliders hamburger joint. Had ¼ pound double cheeseburger. I have dined well thanks to money of a dying woman.

Well, was w/friend—won't say who—we had a big very anti social big argument. –Over an open door! I did not want to go to the place @ first. XX got cold seated beside the open door, so calmly PU plate & moves to another table to continue dining, leaving me sitting there dining alone—in the cold!

In any friendship this would be something considered bizarre, and thoughtless!

PM
Well had stupid fight w/XX; should have known after preaching some spiritual insight to her, there would be a negative reaction— Spoke about the healing power of Communion, of Christ and right after this

26

came our argument. This is not her fault—it is a spiritual thing. The powers of darkness, opposing. The darkness is infuriated at the idea of their captive being loosed. So there, that's about it.

OM had told XX:

> Once you receive a miracle you asked for from God, try to get closer to God, because it will benefit you as a human being. You will have spiritual growth. Take the communion serious and the teachings— its all there to benefit you! Forget the bad teachings of those ignorant churches of the past—try to let it go! Make use of the enlightened teaching here, and their very accepting views!

Learn & grow while you are able!

Monday, December 30
Placing hate into the trash is a refreshing shower! Clean!

XX (MTF) was: *consolidating everything in my small studio apartment. Throwing out furniture—but the paper—*(her art-of-sorts—her passion on paper), *this must be saved!* A life's work! Is culling thru her small space (300 square feet) threw all furniture out: *It's the papers.*

Condensing in this space a lifetime of paper work– into a storage locker in a small town in the Bay Area, outside the selfish, greedy city of SF. Like all of us, consciously, or unconsciously, she is preparing to move if she is forced to.

> We get to this point in our life, its time to turn inward. At this time there's a check due us—a big paycheck. Its time to cash the check— or it'll go bad on you.

Headlines:

> TEACHERS FORCE TO FLEE SF'S HIGH RENT
> —Long Commute Hours means Less Time Spent w/Students

Any change in our environment—like a giant throws a big boulder into a pond —sets into motion unexpected results; displaces the

27

customary inhabitants; aliens enter the environment speaking foreign tongues; things in disarray making ill-feelings.

Am @ Hos. Sun setting over horizon grey/pink just as many winters in every big city.

My world is more silent now—earlier spoke w/Gary & Rich— now sit alone. Along comes XX who is physically declining, saw that @ church last nite. Life ain't easy.

My clue to leave is when the sun goes down.

Well, re: last nite, when 2 abused people try to be friends it requires a lot of work. If this work is not done only greater love will sustain the relationship.

He studies human & pigeon behavior in the Ho's parking lot. Birds— pigeons fly. Children —us advanced apes—stomp. They love to jump up/down—delighting in their ability to create a loud noise.

So @ our age it is time to be reflective, to look into yourself.

PM
Surely your miserable life may be a gift.

His jerkoff was certainly a relief.

Between focusing on computer, CLOSER TO THE HOUR –1 using his one good eye, the OM, caught snippets of TV—where an exploratory ship The Stostkosvki was stuck in the ice @ North Pole. He thought how 100-years ago the famous explorer went to the North Pole, now, mining expeditions are following in the trail he made. Oil well rigs. Messing up the environment, bisecting it w/lines, roads—destroying the home of penguins, polar bears, and elk.

When students and artists go to live in the ghetto, redevelopers, venture realtors, follow; —destroying it for the ethic poor.

As do the heavenly missionaries who are on fire to bring the Word to the savage nations—so the land-grabbing Colonialists can follow in their footsteps to enslave these new converts.

What shit.

It is a fact that quite often @ Coyote—as the sun, bright, moves across the sky warming us utterly, it comes to a sky-high block—the greedy 12-story rich peoples condo building newly constructed—and now the light and the warmth are blocked to us for a period of 45 minutes, before the sun traverses to the other side of this obstacle –the sun, multimillion miles off in distant perspective—and therein lasts a short while longer before it descends, falling beyond earth's edge. So it is this 45 minutes of extra warmth and light we are robbed of—by the rich kkkapitalists!

As still wearing that tie from Dan—the brown one.

I am conducting a search—for the billionth time, excruciating. — To fill book order.

I believe I will discontinue my original DOING IT FOR THE MISTRESS, (Gay, Lesbian, Bisexual, Transsexual F*ck Stories) and just issue the Text POD version, on Amazon. So much less work then building the goddamn book from nothing but a photocopied master page.

Tuesday, December 31, New Years Eve!
Call from Monsieur Hugo—to meet on Polk Strassa.

Got to Coyote early—surprise, no one out here but its open till 11PM— real business hours.

Hugo was frustrated, as so many, by the over high priced cost to park his truck—25¢ per quarter-minute—which is a fortune just to go and dine. He drove round and round, finally PU me and we head out!

We talked about the aging process and how our bodies are falling apart:

29

Genetic information has been copied so much by now its full of mistakes. Our DNA replicates itself to make us like we were; its goal is to replicate ourselves exactly as in the beginning; it cleans up everything again and again. As we age it doesn't copy itself as well. That's why when we get old we stop looking like ourselves so much.

Out w/Monsieur Hugo—we drove to beach surveyed Pacific Ocean, best way to begin the New Year.

Of course we returned down past Clement Street, dined on Chinee food— Szechwan – *Van Nuys!*

As you know I am down to the wire w/$. Oh! As Hugo & I are dining, phone call from Dalora to say:

> You have $1,000! It's owed to you by some bank! From XX Avenue—the old house—in XX!

So I have $ coming! $ stolen from us by the banks.

Hugo and I stopped by the bookstore there. We headed thru the dusty rows, up the home-built wooden steps to the 2nd floor; old site of their GLBT section—alas it has been no more for quite a while:

> It was gone last time we were up here!

> Maybe its been dissolved into the ordinary shelves—

> Maybe its by alphabet—that would be a disaster.

> Its gone. —It's moved somewhere else.

Hugo and I discussed women's lib bookstores, and the small bookstores in general—as usual—how they have slowly atrophied into disappearance.

> We don't even have a shelf in Green Apple bookstore any more.

Life/Death—Rebirth. Water is the soul of the earth.

30

Party on TV; loud BOOMS outdoors in the New Years night.

The sky; the real display across the bay; shown in scenes on TV; spiraling—bright fireworks.

Late that night TM discovered a wonderful historical bible Jesus documentary.

Jesus died around 30 ACE, by a fluke of the calendar.

It is New Years 2014.

Around 70 ACE, when the temple in Jerusalem was destroyed the Jews lost their center—they had to think—*what should we do? Where should we go? What does God want us to do?*

This is somewhat like our position here in SF—will we have to leave? Our gay capital has been exploded apart due to high rents; queers are leaving their protective bubble, the dreamland, the promise land, for parts unknown of the USA if not the world.

I want to talk of what I knew thru the dike words I wrote those long years (1963-2000).

PM
Nada.

He stayed up very early @ morning; ears hungry for knowledge.

Watching TV program on Public Broadcast Station —Jesus, Jews/Christians.

Forces that opposed the fledgling religion.

Things darker & deeper.

Wednesday, January 1
Some of the boys are gone—from Miss Polk Strassa—as you know— they may come back months, days, years later—or they are dead. This is how the life is. It's how it was down on the Ho Stroll 1974-

1975, when I was just a young he-she of 35, courtier of the ladies of the evening.

Now it is the boys of ill repute.

Per notification from Gary, went to the alley above Polk, found Junior laying on the sidewalk, asleep. This handsome youth already scars upon his face; expensive clothes, shoes on his perfect body, dusty from street-sleep. Grouchy:

> I hurt all over! I hurt all over my body! I hurt because I'm not high! I need drugs!

Coyote. Mellow jazz plays. Sun shines bright.

Grumpy Junior sprawled out in alley w/dusty clothes.

He is a drug addict. Gave Junior $2 in change & he's been gone extremely too long—can you buy drugs w/only $2? Now am waiting for *Gadot* once again:

> Liza (w/Dog)
> Junior
> God

Things are obvious on this planet—what you truly think about someone or something; it becomes apparent when you do not go to their party but you are obvious by your absence. What you do, what you say, what you fail to do all shows up the same as what you aren't saying!

Well concerning this other being, from the other nite; it is the ME show all about ME; so self-absorbed round & round like a mouse on a wheel—w/all that energy they could be doing something for good.

Outsiders view: So many figures huddled in the sidewalk here & there, in different places. Look down an alley, there is one covered in blanket—look here beside a tenement's brick wall huddled on a piece of cardboard, humans, sleeping.

Here is one of these people down on one knee fidgeting w/their stuff; items from several backpacks spilled out over cold concrete; in a drug stupor, fidgeting, playing w/bright colored pieces of metal.

Saw D— (OGM):

> I just saw Junior, he's up there, suppose to meet him later.

> Oh I just saw XX (his boy), we spent some time together.

It is understood when two older men are speaking @ table, and a young, cute man shows up—trade—that by respect the previous conversation is interrupted w/no excuse nor apology, because *sex comes first!*

The OM was heading home. He spent his last coins on food for the nite @ convenience store.

Church bells called from the cathedral but there was no one to come:

> BONG BONG BONG BONG

It was 4PM.

PM
Well I guess I really proved I am not a hustler—the other nite, when I got mad @ XX thus jeopardizing a friendship (apparently risking it!) which is feeding moi & driving me around in style! A smooth operator allows no such mishaps—because their goal, their intent, is not the mark's (victim) friendship @ all—but their money, or something they have!

Oh, as the evening stands am still waiting to see if XX will call and maybe drive me to Safeway—if not hopefully Jasmin will be well and can keep our preset suggested appointment tomorrow to do some of her Home Health Care chores for me. AND, am waiting to see if Junior will find a phone & still have my phone number, and call me tonight after 10—as suggested, so he can come over here & sleep part of the night & maybe eat. —And beat his meat! YUM!

Have been letting parrots out more now since been recovering. Feel their hot little pink & grey-specked feet on my shoulders.

Hot feathers against my skin. Chortling in my ear. Pecking around my neck and hairline.

Needless to say it is almost 1AM, Junior is a no-sho.

Women sit in pew of church on TV, solemn, in all piety; hats set on their heads in a drunken angle.

Oh, Jasmin is not sure if she can come over tomorrow or Friday. I have no money and little food—but a $50 Safeway Card! Seems XX isn't going to help by driving me there. Actually now it is Miss Jasmin's *duty,* according to her new job doing *Home Assistance* pour moi!

> Can you drive me to the Safeway store tomorrow?
>
> I thought I was coming over to talk about filling out the forms for my paycheck!
>
> Well I need someone to drive me to the Safeway.
>
> Can you take the BART subway over here?
>
> WHAT!
>
> Oh…
>
> If I take the subway over there—how can I bring my laundry? Where is my clean laundry you did!
>
> Oh, I forgot about that…

So you see how this thing is going… already… AURRRUGHH!!!!

So looks like I'll have to take bus over to Safeway just for food to eat, to supplement the Meals On Wheels until my Foodstamps activate the nite of Jan 4th! Whenever I take the bus it's hard to bring home big items, that a car can do best!

Café. A 4-Brush/1-Pallet Knife nite.

Thursday, January 2
Coyote—Gary sez Cosmo sightings:

> He called from the discount store; he was probably stocking his car
> w/socks, underwear, & cigarettes, for the boys.

Times moves on in procession like Grace Cathedral's High Service
w/smoke, bells, whistles.

Junior appeared looking very nice in a suit, carrying backpack—he is
out to make some rounds tonite—probably drug currier— said he
might stop by since he was going to be in my neighborhood; he did
not call.

Junior said something awful, which pissed me off:

> Stop talking like a woman!

What in hell am I doing wrong? Has someone told him my TG
status? Is he reading me, w/out knowing! This is so aggravating!

Get serious desperate troubled calls. —From XX, immigration shit.
From Jasmin—going to court over a bill collector. Aurughh…

Saw Wayne in front of Gay Men's theatre; he looked good. I'm glad
he is beginning a new alternate career as a waiter, while the former
one as a dancer begins to grow old. As we talked in the open air a
handsome gay man passed; we stood together, the man devouring
Wayne w/his eyes.

> By the time this ordeal is over I'm ready to retire to the psychiatric
> institution. That's my retirement plan.
> --XX

> 2 bad Immigration doesn't allow inter-species marriages! I'll have 5
> husbands! I'll get humped by 5-nice furry & feathery mice/bird
> husbands.
> --XX

What a vivid imagination!

> Oh my God why is my life like this? Its so fucked up! What have I done in my past life?

Flying hell, hellish hell.

Just the 2nd day of the New Years & its already problems.

PM
Suddenly the OM realized he'd taken on the problems of 3 people:

> Jasmin—in court for money owed
> XX—immigration snafu
> Junior—dopedealing

None of these missteps were his own! He, himself had recently emerged from:

> Penny Cats illness & transition to Cat/People heaven
> Medical snafu
> Dust mite infestation
> Insufficient money to be worked out into a budget

Friday, January 3
Headlines newspaper:

BIG FIGHT AMID BOOM
Battles Over Buildings Could Explode As City Works To House
Residents Projected To Move Here In Future Housing

***

Uber Livery Service Kills A Girl In The Downtown Streets

—Uber is one of the yuppies upscale cab services. So you see mega troubles are being created in our Grand Dame of a city by these recent, heartless upscale émigrés.

@ Coyote; Singing Man, Rich, & Gary, soon left & I'm on my wei.

These messed up—born into unholy homes, mental illness, afflicted w/drunks, dope; grown up broken & have to repair themselves…

Am certainly glad am a customer once more —@ Coyote; tho being RENT day I have no $ to spend on cafè—& make this official.

The OM gave what he spied on sidewalk a tap w/cane; it turned out to be a yellow/brown-speckled banana peel—response was so light—meaning no banana meat was inside. He knew @ once it was empty.

Oh, did I tell you found a book by Octavia Butler—Parable Of The Talents. She is now deceased. Have grown to like this author, blax feminist. She is science fiction genre—on recommendation of Monsieur Hugo.

As known, Octavia won a spectacular award a few years before her death, w/these monies was able to buy a house in semi isolation in Seattle. It was partially the cause of her death when she suffered a stroke, and fell down outside on the land, hitting her head on a rock and dying in a diabetic coma—no one was around to see—who could have saved her.

Sat in Ho's lot—there saw billboard ad for spooky motion pix, Paranormal Activity. Know XX will relish this—seems some mental people gravitate to space aliens, and out-of-this-world realities, as some kind of hope for their messed-up lives.

Saw Vick Lee from TV station, shook his hand. He was there on corner of Hyde & Bush doing a story on two pedestrians who had been hit/killed by cars on this day alone—one in the morning, the 2nd just hours ago.

All this is madness venture kapitalism—driving around in fast new cars crazy; result of a global wealth city too busy gouging out dollars; and old people trying to pick our way thru it.

Now seated outside in the nite on fire hydrant, waiting for Annie Ho to PU me & drive me to pay my RENT. Outside in front, cars come & go, hundreds of people.

Watch for those who walk along the margins beside the gutters looking for castoff cigarette butts.

> When I first got to Grace Cathedral I kept waiting for them to talk about the devil, about hell, about demons, about Satan, Lucifer, & how you're going to hell! & never heard it. I'd kept waiting for it. I'm shocked—something is really wrong, something is missing @ Grace Cathedral!

PM
Nada.

Saturday, January 4
Sat now in sun of Coyote. Jasmin dropped him off.

She came baring his laundry & a sandwich. They talked about her forthcoming job working for him & getting paid, doing stuff she's already been doing but not getting paid. She picked up an immense bag of laundry in replace of the two, clean, & neatly folded, she had returned.

On wei to church Installation of Caren as priest, then reception (food!). Glorious day out—sun.

OM thought it was a good thing not see Junior & take him to the Instillation for food—*I've already messed up a wedding—not this too! Bringing asinine friends to nice events.* It was all in his ongoing quest to save souls. I recall:

> He had invited 2 black dikes of the underclass, acquaintances of his from the nightclub. Two bulldagger hypes. One hundred guests were in attendance. The TV news had come to the wedding because of its unusuallity, & were filming—two women marrying each other, one blax one white. It was 1975. It was a Christian wedding. Suddenly there was an announcement—the wedding was halted; it was to inform the guests if they had left any purses or wallets along w/their coats down in the guest room, they should go there immediately to see if they had been stolen. The two hypes had been caught down there rifling thru coat pockets & purses!

38

Saw Olde Jolly and we talked.

What's this? Says Olde, he saw a cute man @ next table; *is that a sexchange?* He wants to know. He saw another cute man: *will I fit in there? I wonder...* he says.

We talked about a sex worker in the East Bay who you call on the phone and he'll come PU you @ the BART subway station.

All these arrangements...

> I've had him.

> He doesn't want to do anything.

> He won't do hardly anything in bed.

Politely walked beside, waited for him to shuffle-step to the WallGrims—we take 20 minutes to go 2 blocks!

> I should have taken the bus.
> --Olde

> How do you feel?

> I feel like a trick.

> ***

> On one of his tours thru the club Red is propositioned by a freak.

> "No, I'm not interested."

> He tries again. Does Red appeal to the freak as a fag, a dike, a tranny? An SM player? What?

Along California Street roots of the trees were breaking up the sidewalk—nature would not stop—& destroyed this temporal stuff humanity builds. The old man quickly stumbled up the road.

Vesting in the vestry w/their transvestments.

Finally, beloved, whatever is true, whatever is honorable, whatever is just, whatever is pure, whatever is pleasing, whatever is commendable, if there is any excellence and if there is anything worthy of praise, think about these things. Keep on doing the things that you have learned and received and heard and seen in me, and the God of peace will be with you.
--Philippians 4:4-9

OM had cussed God out royally the day of the Installation w/a huge temper tantrum. He was so angry, discontent, frustrated, uncertain; his seeking unfulfilled.

OM's collar was sweating on his neck. He looked up & there, beside the alter, as if in a mirage, some of the gone clergy was miraculously returned—for a moment— come to give their support for the newly installed Priest(ess). All the priests were dressed in white robes w/red transvestments—Holy music bellowed melodic from the organ—*it will be stilled.*

So what do I do for the time when the organ is stilled? —Words & deeds for the future!

During this high service a voice would arise & T was startled, would look around to see where it came from; w/sound system disorientating him as does in a sonic boom that breaks the sound barrier, when you see a plane flying faster then the speed of sound, but no sound accompanies it until moments later.

The pew he sat in was built for the choir to open their sheet music upon, so it was like a lectern.

On the alter they introduced a female speaker, a priest, who spoke of her partner—a woman— how holistic their lives seemed, where as out in the street its drink, pills, trade, solitary lives afraid to trust.

The church is the family of God.

Will you preserve in prayer for yourselves & others!

The Spirit.

Venti sancti spiritu.

The clergy assembles from all parts of the congregation to lay hands upon the new priest being made.

Venti sancta spiritu.

They went into a huddle, hands-on.

There, beside the alter he saw something!

Something new!

He was jealous! Jealous! Now he saw it! All his banter, his sarcasm, his tearing them down to size! For he had not yet received his own position! His deserved acclaim!

So that was the key to his attitude! *I should have known! Jealously!* He who wasn't very much jealous of anybody.

T had to cast it out of his life immediately—but not into the hate bucket—a new place! God was showing him a new place! Jealousy!

He had eaten the communion.

You have dined well!

You will be great Red Jordan –you will put out many ministers in My Name.

The OM had gone past his fork in the road—& now was going along the right way.

PM
I believe the children of God(ess)'s creation believe in God—but they know little about Her/Him & hate, despise Her wretched church which has become outdated, does not serve them at best, and giving them false instructions for the suppression of females, blacks, the

uneducated et al; which has been a tool of oppression for century upon century— @ worst; collaborator w/warriors who conquer & oppress, robbers stealing the last sou from the poor; lovers in bed w/Mafia, Medici, nobility et al, and all the things of earth which are powerful—when in fact their duties—as spelled out by J.E.S.U.S. C.H.R.I.S.T. in the gospels of the Holy Bible says to do just the opposite!

> Give to the poor
> Tend to the week, the brokenhearted!
> Protect the landless widows & give them shelter!

Ha! Ha! Ha! These wretched Poops in red gowns, red slippers, & red socks have done little of this and much much more of the dining on fine huge hams, porks, roast beefs, in their monastic hideaways & vestries, such as the classic scene in Doubt, staring Merrill Streep as Mother Superior!

Ha! Ha! Ha!

> Jesus said to them, 'I am the good shepherd. The good shepherd lays down his life for the sheep. The hired hand, who is not the shepherd and does not own the sheep, sees the wolf coming and leaves the sheep and runs away—and the wolf snatches them and scatters them. The hired hand runs away because a hired hand does not care for the sheep. I am the good shepherd. I know my own and my own know me, just as the father knows me and I know the father. And I lay down my life for the sheep. I have other sheep that do not belong to this fold. I must bring them also, and they will listen to my voice. So there will be one flock, one shepherd. For this reason the father loves me, because I lay down my life in order to take it up again. No one takes it from me, but I lay it down of my own accord. I have power to lay it down, and I have power to take it up again. I have received this command from my father.
> --John 10: 11-18

> ***

> We were queer. Searching our identity in a blind, silent Amerika, out of its sin strips and police-raided taverns, finding out we were more then gay—we were born the wrong sex in the wrong body —

herded into police wagons with the other queers denied jobs, kicked out of our birth homes.
--STREET OF DREAMS

RE; our homosexuality—I don't think God would have created us if S/He didn't have use of us. —Watching Cage Au Folles.

Watched Tony Curtis, Marylyn Monroe, Jack Lemon, Joe E. Lewis; SOME LIKE IT HOT!

Sunday, January 5
God is good—but it seems God puts us to the test constantly.

Our new Grand Steps are lovely & pristine. The gold plated stair railings shine.

He huddled up under the comforting arms of Grace, which was supporting him w/small monies/foods & a minimal amount of companionship & big knowledge. Her grey walls lofted; the holy spires & turrets awed; plus the Holy Spirit had spoken to him every single time, furthermore Jesus Christ had appeared to him in a vision, here (place) & gave knowledge (verba) & so his knowledge was of the intellect & the Spirit.

Now he waited for the 6—& to see what wayfarers & fellow travelers might appear.

I Am the Good Shepard.

Tourists were snapping pictures of themselves foolishly, cluttering up the landscape of this holy place.

He awaited to see if A Ho would arrive @ the 6 & prayed he would not have to marry her in order for her to obtain citizenship.

Spoke w/Jasmin she brought over laundry—which she dropped off.

Well it is still a lonely life—I see the lonely.

Jasmin has to PU laundry—I always have laundry—due to dust mites.

Weather was mild—so he sat out in the plaza—heard sound of sloshing fountain:

SLOSH, SLOSH, SLOSH

Red to God: You are bad.

Spirit: God is not bad.

Red: God You are not bad, not one bit, in any way shape or form— it is me who is bad.

Spirit: You're not bad.

Red: There is a bad. The animals are not bad.

Animals: We hate the bad. We are not bad.

All: The bad comes between us.

Cool, on the plaza. Almost deserted. An occasional person.

A freak has come to the fountain. A freak barely clothed. Naked, but for skimpy shorts; a hat, socks & shoes, & earphones. A freak almost naked in this weather, he skips, hops, jumps, runs; does squats. Round & round the geyser fountain.

Oh my God the freak is beginning to sing!

Sing of the fountains of Venice!

The naked freak runs round & around the fountain. –Singing!

Shadows fall over the plaza.

Evening shadows fall on all of us. We pass into the death experience.

The freak does squats, now he is doing a Cha Cha Cha!

Oh my God, what a freak!

A gay Freak!

Transcend. Says the Lord(ess).

He flounces & twists & pirouettes naked! How vain!

I'm having my very own private boy show!

Sunday; alone in the night. OM returned from the loo where he'd spent a penny. The freak was gone, no doubt because he'd lost his audience.

& now our Dean Jane scurries across the courtyard like a mouse—industrious; big glasses; sheaf's of paper in her hand—preparing for her 6-o'clock sermon.

See very dark skin man, contrast to his stark white hair; he's never lonely—he has perpetual people—its built into his culture—from India—for better or for worse they must keep their family from life to death—

OM thanked God for use of his left eye thru which he could see—& earn his living & prays the right will be restored.

All of us higher & lower animals.

A tide of humanity.

He was given a vision in his minds eye—sharp jagged mountain peeks, tremendously high, jagged cliffs, @ violent angles, dangerous; between them is a smooth white winding road that goes *around* & *thru* them… a peaceful life can be had by staying on this road!

The harmonium bellowed & the people sing, *Alleluia!*

Felt presence of God.

He felt happy resting in the hand of God.

On each side of the table-alter were two magnificent floor-length gold candlesticks. A priest stood @ alter; beside him the two grand candles, burning. Suddenly the human-size candlestick seemed so large!

The whole setting surrealistic!

Difference between being in private prayer, and in the middle of an actual church service is like watching a major motion picture on a tiny TV screen or in a huge theatre screen.

OM was catapulted inside of the service, which now transpired as if an angel had opened the Devine Bible, and they were all small children wrapped inside the scriptures!

I'm tired. Tired.

Tired of the old things.

PU aside old things so the new ones can appear.

Jesus; source of all riches.

PM

> I hope he doesn't break her heart.
>
> We all will have to have our hearts broken once or twice before we're done.
> --Downton Abby, PBS TV

God is the only way—other ways are illusion. There is no other way.

Only the experience of age can teach an artist/writer the totality of their work—how to handle it, thru life. In the beginning you are so cautious working and reworking lines, stanzas, phrases. Wiping clean the canvas and beginning over again and again. Over time you accumulate a great body of work. Now you are old. You have multiple copies of texts, master copies, original paintings, and prints of each. How is this going to survive your travels to a smaller room—to a storage locker, which you might visit only two times a year to find & sell a single volume, or a solitary print? What excess baggage can you throw away? What will others make of this storage after you are gone? Will they understand what it is? Each line took an instant to write the inspiration down, so long to figure it out, to change & change again, to work, to re-work, to erase, to add to, to polish, to finish up! How you struggled to compose the painting! To place brushstrokes on canvas, to back away from it & study, to attack, to back off, to close in & complete! Now, all your hard work can be thrown away by mistake!

Monday, January 6
Do basic chores. Kept my household revolving.

Got Meals On Wheels @ front door, very nice, polite, friendly driver, blax lady. Immediately after Jasmin dropped off 2 sacks laundry & PU current large sack laundry. Also gave me $5.

Not seen homeless man in his doorway.

Oh! The dress designer didn't die—but the next-door neighbor hairdresser w/small dog did. Just found out from building manager Sid, there.

Anything we do in this world has an effect. Even the lowest tortured soul who breaks branches off innocent trees—has an effect. All criminals in their crime—for whatever reason, have an effect.

When I was in the female gender I was hard, masculine, made mannish gestures—but after the first few months of transition, my hands began to flounce—as if my gender was counterbalancing itself!

Monsieur Hugo always said that nature seeks a balance, perpetually, so if you are very strongly mannish, after awhile you will turn around and be very strongly female.

PM
Just got my Crank (Bank) Statement. This is so insane—did one of my subtractions bounce? The human race spends its life robbing & stealing from one another. There must be a better way.

Jerk off:

47

Rewind porn video.

Stop video @ scene of sucking a big dick.

Too good to miss! Rewind some more!

Stop @ in/out fucking an orifice! Too Good to Miss! Rewind still more!

Et al!

Went to Mark's Place tavern, there saw Kurt handsome & very nice bartender. OGM there, talking about:

Well my boy is @ home waiting for me!

Well my boy he sees money laying on the street and he goes & gets it and brings it to me...

Turns out they are speaking of their dogs!

RE; my fine arts painting, I lack inspiration—so am praying for it!

Café. A 4-Brush Nite.

Tuesday, January 7

SF ENDS FREE RIDE
FOR TEKKIE'S SHUTTLE

Headlines—hated yuppie rich bus! Tinted windows! Privilege! Gynormous huge busses! Rude, thoughtless, tekkies w/no social training!

So, the city is going to take away their tax break! Good! So many picket lines formed against them, no doubt!

One reason blax people are hated—they are in direct competition w/other po' people. Struggling whites, dirt-po' Chinee, indigent Latin.

Case in point, OM approached end of the block, fully intending to lean up against a street lamp pole while the light made its change—there appeared a slo-walking blax couple—they crossed right in front of him, so he had to stop, hovered on his cane, because they were laboring along so slowly; then, the female leaned tiredly against the post! She beat him to it! And both of them were half his age! Plus they weren't from the neighborhood; *don't even live here!* They were making their weary way uphill to St Francis hospital, to the emergency ward.

Jazz everywhere; marking time w/strident rhythm thru Coyote amplifiers—also jazz on the call waiting of the eye doctors office, as TM waited @ a café table/chair outdoors.

As far as the eye could see, up/down Café frontage, only one sole customer, the blax gentleman who sits in baseball togs ordering a meal & beverage quite often; also some hanger-on, who spends no money.

Where is everybody? It is a decent day & some sun—is it as they say—the most murderous suicidal days—these first days after the holidays are finally ended & everyone is home, blue, nursing their wounds—w/no longer faith in finding anything out in the festival streets which have now dissipated.

A Noise! Large rough blax man staggers down in the street right beside the traffic; hollers, makes threatening gestures—but he moves on.

I sit, ever-hopeful.

Our cook, Ed from Grace goes past—

    Will I see you Thursday @ the Senior's lunch?

    No!

    Oh forgot you're not old enough—

He winks w/a twinkle in his eye.

Truly the OM was young @ heart.

Red Jordan Arobateau
Saturday, January 11, 2014
11:00 PM, Pacific Standard Time
San Francisco, CA

Part- 2

Sky is gray-white haze; sun blotted behind opaque mist so it glows & only occasionally peeks thru bright yellow, blazing—

Face went past which reminds me of a T gal I knew from Trans Space—long ago—maybe she is dead. Or, maybe she lingers here on earth because she had a purpose—a purpose seems to keep us alive longer—she had a website & was going to City College— (If the Greater Powers don't shut that down—as it is a hope for many on the lower rungs of society.)

Sun came out for another moment—brilliant.

Olde in hospital—a stroke. He is disorientated, he doesn't know if it is it the stroke he already had or a new one.

A bizarre drag queen across the street; queen wears a skirt, her hair male cut, short—like the heroine in the Cage Au Folles/Birdcage when her son takes off her wig and declares she is his mother (she raised him) — she wears fishnet stockings & tacky high heels. Panhandling & providing a clown show.

Now a man has approached, normal appearing, he holds her briefly in an embrace, and is giving her kind words. It illustrates how there is someone for every one.

Mellow jazz. So mellow sax.

But when I look back she is alone again, sitting on the street—seated w/all her stuff around, as if that was her home forever.

I am going courting. Have purchased a certain younger gentleman his favorite treat food—French bread & butter. –The bartender in Marks Place.

Am back in Mark's Place seeing the fabulous K—bartender w/the Most-esst.

Face of pain stretched out; cold cold sidewalk on a blanket—gazing up in misery.

TV news; unspeakable ignorance of this case of a woman whose child has died unexpectedly during a routine operation in hospital. This woman refuse to have her child disconnected from life support—tho she has been declared brain-dead by 3 experts. There is these categories:

Comatose
Vegetative state
Brain dead

In the first two there is still life, and brain activity is observed. Some of these categories have returned from their comatose state and regained life once more.

Brain dead people are gone—and they will never come back.

The woman insists God can do a miracle and restore her child—but it is impossible for this to happen, because the child's soul has already ascended to heaven because the body is DEAD!

The woman is grief-struck and is ignorant of medical facts. But the relatives and lawyer surrounding her are possessed by green dollar bills I think, and have a vested interest in playing along w/the mother's denial and grief—for future bucks for all of them.

This is a disturbing situation. It is costing the taxpayers multimillions of dollars and must become the seed for new legislation and rules governing it, because if enough people insisted on keeping corpses hooked up to ventilators & feeding tubes w/round-the-clock nursing, long after they have died it would bankrupt our system.

Medical procedures & facts must be explained to the common folk!

What we are experiencing in our nation weather-wise is an artic vortex—colder days not been seen in a generation, and probably will not return for another generation. The frigid artic air, which usually circulates around the North Pole, has done a sudden dip down dramatically to encompass the lower half of the USA in sub zero temperatures—Chicago is minus -16 degrees. When I lived there as a child it never went lower then 5 or 6 degrees below, and usually might hit 2 or 3 below. In Minnesota –40 degrees.

Artic cold—he wore his Rooski hat, thick & warm w/ear flaps.

> We are into week 2 of the New Years!
> The holiday season is over!
> -Heard on street

More folks @ Hos taking about how people they know are preparing for their removal. Ejecting unnecessary furniture, consolidating books, videos, throwing off stuff they absolutely do not need.

Make way for corporate yups; affluence; must be some changes made in this town to stop this!

The city's soul is hemorrhaging red blood.

I'm not doing it no more—I'm not putting food out there no more—the homeless man is gone.

Dead evergreen trees lying everywhere on their sides, wooden feet upturned in an X. Once green thick boughs; brown. 2 or 3 trees at street corners beside curbs. Next to tenement buildings.

People put up their firewalls. –Protection. Case in point XX never given me her cell phone number—the number she carries about w/her—only her home #.

> I guess I'll hang in there for the safety of my finches & my fish.
> --Annie

PM
Well the species know how to jiggle each other around—two birds preen each other, carefully avoiding the eyes of their companion as they peck and nibble about for mites and dive under the others wing to sort the feathers into place.

Humans know how to jiggle each other's sex parts about—for mutual satisfaction. So isn't this a wonderful plan!

How The Wafer Turns—Kathy's secret code word for the
scandal/gossip @ Grace—of which there is plenty. We say—oh well,
that's just How The Wafer Turns… when some new priest is
beheaded, or staff dismissed or some other actions taken from higher
ups—

This of course is word play on the Old TV Soap Operas—How The
World Turns, etcetera…

Oh, had a prophecy for Annie—delivered it—and she took it very
well. Because it helped her life.

Wednesday, January 8
Well I guess the struggle is part of it. On wei to shrink.

MIDDLE CLASS DISAPPEARING FROM THE CITY

—Newspaper headlines.

The world of men. Sissified older gentleman, polite and very nice,
twinkling eyes, sits next to much younger good-looking youth. His
boy.

Money & security is a component of this relationship.

The homeless blax man who has sat on Van Ness Ave in front of the
Fox Plaza condos was shot and nearly murdered as I reported a while
back. Today heard it from the horse's mouth; the old man himself
covered in blankets of the homeless, in his wheelchair—surrounded
by a panhandling tin can, huge bedroll, a book, stack of Street Sheets
newspapers for sale; donated food in clean proper containers: *You
heard I got shot? He was a blax dude, 6'2": about 240 pounds w/a
white beard.*

His speech is slurred as one suffering brain damage.

Sit here a Coyote's chair—cold sun blotted blind behind white cloud-
fog.

Black voluminous clouds rolling over the sky stark contrast to the white billowing cloud fog.

Oh the Gay Newspaper is back @ Coyote! As you recall the former crazed owner had it taken out.

PM
Big Penis!

Hot jerkoff!

Thursday, January 9
Saw her pix front page 3 BAR—Gay newspaper. Obituary—a public worker; trans gal, divinity student; killed in hit & run accident New Years, Oakland.

> Its great up here Red! You won't believe it!

Red was partial to her—being she was so dark blax—and he hi-yella, and always had an encouraging word for her. Bobbi Jean had a notorious bad temper—but because of his sincere liking, he never saw this side of her directed @ him.

Bobbi Jean Baker, blax gal, Christian.

T gazed out @ the world thru his impacted eye—he could see a bit & he was thankful.

Very delicious warm food. Spice-laden. Pakistani.

Annie & me discussed the fact that the 6PM was moving back —out of the choir loft to the labyrinth in front, beside the baptismal font— and how many of us like meeting back there in the choir loft, very near the large silver Crucifix, which is the centerpiece of the rear wall of the cathedral, but nobody listens to our opinion. Annie said she liked the choir loft better too—

> Because it's a holy place, — a safe place, heart of the church.
> Sanctuary. The whole church is holy but especially there.

If there is a group of red ants, a group of black ants, and a group of regular brown ants, and an ant—say a brown ant— is crippled laying broken on its back, other brown ants will come and attend to it, lift it up and carry it back down into safety in the ant hill, for it to recover. The black ants and red ants will ignore it. Likewise they will save one of their own. But no other species of ant.

It is by scent. They go by scent. If you take an ant and wash it and put it back into the ant hole it will be in trouble, they will kill it.

> They target people who look hopeless, lost, or in trouble. Once when I was younger in Beni Honda restaurant, a woman told me she was reading my aurora, and knew I was in trouble. She saw me and targeted me. They look for people going thru a horrible situation in life, they will go for it.

> Yes, I've heard of that.

> They ask for $20 then $100, then $500—then they say you must give them $2,000 or you are going to die, its critical! You must pay $2,000 within the next 24 hours!

> I've heard of people loosing their homes—to a fortune teller.

> Another time I went into a theatre, it was a paranormal movie, and I got targeted again. This woman came and sat next to me and she talked to me, and she said she had the 6th sense—and offered to give me a psychic reading—*my temple is right down the street*—she says. I went there, she charged me $20 for the reading. But she said: *you really need your aurora cleansed.*

> How much?

> $500.

> Church should start charging people to pray for them under the foot of the Cross, or beside the statue of the Virgin Mary. Each time.

> High prices psychic reading…

> I've heard of it!

57

Now you know someone who has actually experienced it!

Elevate people from suffering into peacefulness. This should be the job of a healer. Not to charge $2,000!

I'd be nice to people & do best not to judge people.

Elevate suffering if you see anybody in pain & suffering.

PM
Nada.

When you are a person driven out of every place it is because you are to become the center of your own place—your own galaxy, your own system.

Friday, January 10
God's Way.

I am @ Hos; sun descending, bright orange/yellow.

I am alone.

Another Christmas tree w/foot upturned in an X. Sun orange dips towards the line of horizon.

Today sat w/Gary & Rich for awhile in the sun.

Oh, did I tell you the horrible news, talked to Cosmo yesterday evening on the phone; he was headed to the airport—flying out to Thailand:

> Joe is back on drugs. He's still out in Modesto, but he's using again.

More news of Olde Jolly in hospital—he has been moved to another hospital. I recall:

> Saw Olde Jolly and we talked. Politely waited for him to shuffle-step to the WallGrims—we take 20 minutes to go 2 blocks!

I should have taken the bus.
--Olde

I recall, in hindsight, that the old guy did not look too good—
somewhat shaky, and a bit more red-faced. Should have realized
something was wrong then. That had been January 4. He had this
stroke 5 days later, on Thursday.

Oh, someone who works for her told me Olde's true name is Bob
Smith—or some ordinary dreck—which does not @ all reflect her gay
spirit. So it was a lie when she told everybody her mother had given
her a woman's name @ birth because they wanted a girl. And in her
younger years she use to walk around in drag—a big muumuu thing;
calling herself what we call her now—XX.

PM
Nada.

Saturday, January 11
Well again I'm nervous & my eye pressure is high.

Others come in here w/family members & my companion Jasmin—
who is now off doing errands.

For L's job big party tonite@ Yacht club.

Beginning to think so many of this world's humans are stupid. A
small percent are brilliant, and many are superior. —It is them who
are the eye doctors, the technicians, of every race, black, Persian,
Chinese, Latin, white.

Step by step it is a processes; doctor procedure begins.

Pressure was high in both eyes today.

It is 12 Noon; sun beginning to brighten the sky.

He ran thru the rolodex of his friends in his mind; knew who would
be by who would not—

So what would be his logical mechanism to live well & leave behind; as others—who give loved children, —magnificent projects that do good for the human race.

The world is my observatory—lay out my paper sheaf on counter top & write my wisdom while the world passes by outside on Polk Street. Singing Man walked past stopped in said hello. 1st hour I sat there half asleep, and finally woke up.

PM
Nada.

Sunday, January 12
Oh my God it was so hard, so difficult, so afraid, —running in the street after my own queer people—approaching God, having no idea of this.

It was in winter, in snow on the ground over stubbled fields; smoke rising from chimneys…

The cathedral was full of suited men—suits/w/ties. There was a recital.

Women dressed worthy of mention in $ money, —for the recital

Preppies in blue blazers, khakis trousers; red ties. They trooped into the vestry door—it was locked against them. He had to: *remove the hate from your heart to approach Me.* Lit his candle.

Sweat rolled off his back under his great green coat & plaid shirt from climbing the hill.

The alter was clothed in rich red/white robes; himself, he felt ragged.

The congregants were a school of fish under the dangling dazzling streamers like water hung from the ceiling of the cathedral 7 floors above.

Murderous scream—of the little girl-child to be baptized!

Had no idea the human race was so loud!

Blood curdling, screaming voice!

That was some serious screaming. So many horrors; moving, screaming.

Glass w/bullet hole front windowpane has been removed & replaced clean pure glass. Delicious aromas. Pakistani food. Have not eaten all day. Jasmin to PU early tomorrow for eye doc.

A & I spoke of the image we believe others have of us @ the church:

> I wouldn't be surprised if they if they thought we were losers. Look! There go the loser friends!

> They judge on physicality, superficial physicality.

We spoke of the little girl-child's baptism:

> Most lively most exciting baptism service ever!

> ***

> In the end we can't even keep our own bodies. All that makes any difference, it's how we treat each other that counts.

> After this is all over & I go on to heaven & am going to demand of God — why all this hell I had to go thru!?

PM
A young girl has escaped the male dominated Alcaida hate murderous forces, in her country of Afghanistan. Her brother & another brutish man are Taliban generals and they forced her to wear the suicide vest. She was to blow herself up in a police station to kill the police. She got out of the situation and has turned herself into the police & asking for amnesty.

One cannot look at the female bodies clothed head to toe in burkas— burlap robes like sacks covering their entire being—and not see they are made into slaves. Where is the human rights outcry? Violence against women has escalated 25% since the USA began withdrawing our troops—and regions we once secured for freedom have been overtaken once again by the murderous barbarians. Women are enslaved, murdered, mutilated w/impunity. Women's noses and lips cut off by the male Taliban fill the hospital. A genocide against females has been declared. The burn unit houses women w/swathes of bandages over their faces arms & upper bodies where they have attempted to self-immolate themselves—kill themselves—to escape their horrendous slave fate.

The world must do something!

The position of women is now worse then it was before the USA invaded!

This world is as close to hell as some of us will get.

Monday, January 13
Am @ eye clinic it is so busy. Early. Jasmin PU me.

Well. I am too fat & know this is my problem.

Sold 2 books, 1 borrowed, so far this month, including 1 CHINA GIRL.

Hurrah! Call from friend; Native American dental—Medical is paying senior's dental once again!

Do not judge—let me met out justice—says the Lord.

Felt pretty horrible after excruciating morning—eye worry—Jasmin well-got me to clinic before time; saw the glaucoma doctor who said my eyes look good, no glaucoma—those drops Dr. Asher gave me dropped my eye pressure from a horrible 23, 25, down to 13, 11! Talked to Gary later who says he's taken the drops for 30 years.

Got up that AM w/no sleep practically—Jasmin call me wake up & disregarded it—then her 2nd call was to say she was on her way and I was not yet up! Had just started getting up & she was there in my doorway! Staggered out—torture in waiting room from no sleep & worry but found out eyes looking better on all fronts—also a tiny shred more of sight has returned to right eye: *if its not getting any*

62

worse we count that as better! Says doc, plus it is getting slightly better.

Got my 3 or 4th eye shot, now to see if any improvements, tho miniscule, follow. Jasmin came @ good time drove me home, while I waited the Native American Dental rescheduled me, and PAWS said they'd be by with cat/bird food. Am saving C-food for when another beast makes its way to my home once again.

Laid down in bed around 11 to sleep—shortly the Roach man came by, put poison in kitchen to kill roaches. Shortly later Meals On Wheels arrived w/supply of food. Slept some more and then up to make it out to sun and fellow OGM's and maybe a boy toy….

Sat in sun and talked, G. senior brought me a coffee. I begun to come back to life—but eye itching and itching—forgot to take the anti-itch medicine which helps vastly after a shot.

Wound up in the Hos, talked to Denis and others, then on wei home. Slept. Writing these NOTES. Am coming back to life—w/hope for my sight and am thankful to the Lord(ess).

PM
Prepared canvas for a vision. All red. —Alizarin Crimson Hue.

So far only this red background has been given me. – 20″ X 32″. A 1-Brush Nite.

Tuesday, January 14
Feel out of whack this AM—is it the new eye drops to reduce pressure in my eyes? (25/26 before—even after Lazar drilling holes in them, 11/13 w/drops—Vey Nysse.) Timolol. –It works so is effective.

God has given me a vision of a red canvas; I am obedient. Will cover again w/more red tonite or real soon.

Righteous music @ Coyote but I must move on.

I struggled. I won!

Olde Jolly he such a dirty old man—you can't help but admire that!

Am in Pakistani restaurant. Umgali.

We went and dined on sweet roll & coffee—then went home.

PM
Wrapped 2nd package—for Bancroft. Did Amazon package the other day—BARS HEAVEN order.

Excellent analysis of the Middle East—the corruption against the lower classes is so immense none of them can get ahead. Their law is so archaic that 97% of citizens of Tunisia, Libya, & Iraq do not hold legal deeds to their property—despite owning them. There are no business licenses nor any kinds of advanced banking, nor commerce for any other then the upper classes—who need them the least!

> Many intelligent street survivors who have many a tall tale to tell; they are raconteurs, but not writers.
> --DIFFICULT JOURNEY

Yes, they spin many a tall tale—see them, colorful, obscene, boldly energized, fearless—but their words are lost the moment we gather it into our ears—it is unrecorded anywhere.

Oh, while editing DIFFICULT JOURNEY see much talking about RENT day; exactly rent and no money for treats—but my new budget observance has paid off, plus the new gifts given to me fo' being a po' senior—so I have a small amount of cash left over and over $120 in foodstamps so my former poverty is dissipated!

> Let your light shine. Might be someone down in the valley trying to get home.

Well this is the purpose of my works, and my painting.

News, French TV; another gang rape in India, —of Danish tourist, by 6 men. 52-year old female.
.

She has fled back home to Denmark, but says she will return to India to give testimony in the courts!

Hang the dogs to death from the highest tree!

India, & the world must come to a resolution of the safety of women!

The great Satan is to be without feeling regarding these matters.

Wednesday, January 15
Well came out here @ Coyote—writing first NOTES of the day. Had found 25¢, then 10¢ in the new parking meters coin return slot, then $2 dollar bills, –beside people waiting @ bus stop.

Oh, when headed out had found 1-doz hard-boiled eggs outside fancy tourist hotel.

Nobody out here but 2nd Lady w/Dog.

She asks about Junior but knows nothing.

Well the hot sun is blazing—but cool blows underneath.

The reading lesbian trans woman I know speaks of going to Israel. She is a converted Jew, like many. She is back going to synagogue. She repeats what I first thought of years back:

> The TV doctor says, why bother w/those crossword puzzles; the best way to keep your memory up is to learn a 2nd language.

Gave homeless man collapsed on street I passed by half of the hardboiled eggs found in front of hotel this early afternoon—they are still good.

You must know that you will be opposed.

Am in a jollier mood these days, could be that someone is doing my infernal laundry? Not that Jasmin doesn't like doing it either! But she gets paid to do it!

65

Must say that XX from church who has a habit of yelling @ people when he talks, and I have somewhat escalated our reaction to each other—when he yells @ me, I fight back @ him which infuriates him! Over nothing! And he turns red-faced! Blue eyes blazing. So today was 2nd day in a row I yelled back @ him—not sure how to handle this. –But prayer.

Oh, and another problem may be brewing w/Jasmin & my laundry. Maybe L is pissed @ all these laundry sacks walking up the stairs into their home.

PM
6-billion dollars being raised for Syria—half of their population is in dire need. The civil war there has uprooted them from their land, from their marketplaces—they have no way to earn a living, nor scratch food out of the soil—they are starving, homeless, w/out medical aid.

Troubling situations on TV.

The world is walking by every day—join them? Or join God!

Meld a part of God's DNA into my own DNA.

Thursday, January 16
He stood in front of his building—traffic flowed—honking @ itself. Red, yellow, blue, orange, purple; it was comforting to see a gay flag hanging from the Men's Sex Theatre.

Most foot traffic was walking on its way downtown to the financial destruct.

Driving madly to get to eye doctor apt. Now wait in waiting room to be called.

Oh be so glad to sit in the sun @ last w/coffee & gay friends.

Sat sun blazing down. Très hot.

He followed the sun from chair to chair.

Ha ha ha! Another archival joke—the race down to the wire:

> Trinity church was damaged during the 1989 Loma Prieta
> earthquake as was St. Bridget's – Catholic– over on Van Ness, and
> the City declared both churches must be earthquake retrofitted, or
> they cannot be used for congregations. The diocese decided they
> might as well tear down old Trinity and sell the valuable lot to a
> condo developer, thus enriching the Diocesan coffers by multi-
> millions. The only problem is, Trinity is not just any church—it
> may be the first Episcopal Church established in California, which
> would make it a landmark heritage at least to the Episcopalians—
> and that is the question. It is thought that the magnificent Grace
> Cathedral is the first church established in the California diocese—
> yet there is a hair raising split decision on the matter; Grace Church
> as it was called back then in 1886, was set to be founded, first, and a
> bishop was sent for to establish it officially. A short time later
> Trinity was set to be founded, and a different bishop was called for.
> Grace was called first—but her bishop came late! He decided to
> take the long route round from the East coast—by ship down the
> continent past South America, around the Cape Horn, and back up
> along the western United States. A very lengthy, but well-
> established route. Meanwhile the bishop sent to found Trinity
> decided to risk things and get on that new invention the iron
> horse—the railroad—and steam his way directly across the USA---
> and by this shorter, direct passage arrived at Trinity and founded it
> for the diocese much earlier the Grace. So you see there is
> somewhat of a contest as to which building is officially older. If
> Trinity is older, it will be more elevated in opinion; it will be far
> more difficult to level to the ground and sell off to the highest
> bidder! Ha ha ha!

Homeless Crack hag tries to pry coin out of parking meter; cigarette
smoldering in her bony fingers.

Got Grace check—Yeah!

Wait for Annie Ho, want to go by KKKoporate Kopy Kenter to order
books—

PM

People want to revoke immigration they want to drive you to the absolute end of the world. They are so hateful.

Now we are in amazing Burmese restaurant, first time.

Thank you God.

Nearly closing, late & the restaurant is clearing out.

@ the entrance of this Burmese Restaurant is the standard Shrine w/Buddha in gold in the prayer position, a tribute of fresh fruit in bowls, fresh flowers in jars.

Well horrible little nasty incident happened in 24-hour donut shop— and won't go back there again!

Think some of it is inability to understand English as well. —On the part of the Chinese punk who was serving @ the counter.

Somehow, by mutual fault the OM was served an apple turnover rather then his customary cherry turnover, by the older employee. He was pissed. He told the punk could he have a cherry turnover instead—for half price. Went and put the partially nibbled apple turnover up on the countertop; not rudely, just putting it away like garbage—the same as have put away other garbage in that store. I sat @ my table drinking coffee; punk said he'd see about it—and nothing happened, dawned on me that he wasn't going to ask about anything. But at this point a certain individual decided they would go over to the counter and buy another donut—which pissed me off & I told them not to do this—took the damn thing & put it back up on the counter, but they got it and brought it back over to me.

At this point I started walking out of the store.

Said: *it's a 2 way street buddy*, which is not an attacking thing to say.

At this point I went and stood outside the store and the punk is yelling GET OUT OF MY STORE!

I'm not in your store!

68

> One punch old man, and I'll knock you out!
>
> If you punch me you'll go to jail. You'll go to jail for a long time!
>
> One punch old man!
>
> And you will go to jail for a long time!

Plus I could sue the idiot, and maybe jeopardize his stupid menial job.

Hate this kind of stuff because it makes me feel weak.

See once again how the language barrier is a problem. The stupid young punk might not actually have fully realized what I was saying!

Friday, January 17, (Shabbat)
On his way down street that day who should OM encounter but Miss Daisy, union head honcho and blax activist:

> Have you heard? Did you get the letter? Everybody should have got their letter by now! They're trying to tear down the Balmoral hotel and build a giant condo there!

This was horrible—many poor, decent working poor and retired seniors & also those newly Ellis-evicted from their apartment units by greedy profiteers—had found refuge in the low cost SRO, Balmoral!

Sun bright, Coyote—hot—but when sun dips beyond the egregious kkkorporate konstructs of anti-compassion buildings, we feel @ last the shade & the cold that goes w/that; the sad & sorry state of this affair is that the Most High Lord(ess) God—the Eternal has instructed me that all shall be spoken to, *all*—even the rich.

So as Miss Daisy has informed me—2 two places of refuge for the poor have been slated to be acquired, flipped, yes.

The OM basked in warm light of the sun.

The sun which God(ess) had created & given for us for us tiny desperate angry furry little human *beings*.

The pigeon pecked for food @ his feet; grey white black very energetic, red 4-toed like his human hands.

Now the magnificent sun was being blocked because of a monstrosity 12-story of grey cement.

Blocking it as it floated behind the cubicle-shape building.

The rich are in a world of their own—sometimes one will take on the problems of the poor—and stoop down, become engaged in the muck/mire of their world—to set things straight.

A white girl, blond—nice dressed, tall, intelligent looking—but she carries a tell-tale backpack— is walking fast down the street, spies something—turns out of her way, picks up some papers St Joan has left on her table—for only a moment to come & talk to Red.

The Saint rushes over screaming NO NO! THOSE ARE MINE! And the girl relinquishes them, and passes quickly on down the line.

@ the Hos—sun blazed bright warm but cool wind blows under it.

Seated in Hos there is a hard rough black man who comes here to sit & scream into his cell phone.

Wait for the rest of the crew to arrive—Denis, & the Malaysian, from Grace; the taller white man, ex-hippy, who is the Malaysian's friend.

I had lived a lonely & isolated life—waiting for joy.

Am now going to briefly tell the story of Bishop Pike as it has been told to me, by a certain party from Grace.

Have told you this before—if a person is say, 60-years of age, they will have their memories and some of the memories of the generation, which preceded them—

People of a generation remember their lives, and some of the generation which came before them because they will have their own memories and stories and have heard some memories & tales told to them from their parents times, the things their parents recount from their own childhoods and even of their parents-parents, told to them which would stretch the memory back 2 more generations—.
—DIFFICULT JOURNEY

All these stories buried in the cement of the foundation of Grace; witnesses are all dying out, as the last living members go to the grave. They are old enough to have lived thru it! They know where all the bodies are buried!

Here is the tail of Bishop Pike:

Bishop Pike was a very iconoclastic Bishop, and he got himself into hot water among some of the stodgy pillars of the church.

He was revolutionary from the start—but after his gay son committed suicide—@ a young age—back in a dark time when everyone outcasted gays, — the Bishop stepped off into the deep end.

I suppose he was casting a greater net to try to communicate w/his dead son—he was practicing the occult, consulting séances, working ouijee boards, bringing in fortune tellers; yet all the time dressed in his holy robes w/a giant gold crucifix around his neck, the high bishops hat, & carrying that large staff w/the crook; being a practicing bishop of the cathedral & the entire Northern California diocese. Well this made him a heretic according to the laws of the church! However he was a Bishop! How to get rid of him! No one in the church is higher then the Bishop, you have to go to the Bishops Board, or the Standing Committee—and it was them who put him on trial for heresy! –On 4 counts!

Meanwhile, in the greater community the Bishop was having an effect. The news of what he was doing had begun to leek out to the common world. Many people listened to him, and because of him, due to curiosity; they came back into the church. I was among them.

71

One of the charges was that he had failed to keep the Feast of the Annunciation service, which is a once per year event; and so he was hauled into court—but the keeper of the records brought in the book; he opens the big book—a log of all attendant @ services, w/all the signatures of those clergy in attendance, and there was his name, my name—XX—and Pike's name! So they had to acquit him of that one!

Bishop Pike resigned. Previously he had been tried for heresy—he was tried 4 times. He was acquitted on all of the charges. Shortly after this he resigned his post, and went off to Israel. —Where he accidentally met his demise, by getting lost in the desert.

The people liked him, and he had begun a stir out in the general population who began to hear of him—because of all the scandal bubbling out abut him in church—and people thoroughly not interested in Christian Religion, were beginning to take note.

PM
Wounded.

Well I had been wounded by the incident the other day—and the Lord(ess) told me so.

Got to my house, went into kitchen; saw the water pitcher & juicer sparkling & twinkling.

Clean, nice smells; this house cleaning service given him, but he was still not happy—alone. But he realized, it was: *so you will not be so taxed.* It was to make my life easier. & to reward Jasmin, who still needs a job, and must labor for the rest of her working years—12 more to go till age 62.

Well white people have ruled the globe for over a millennium—now it is time for them to step along side of others of us…

Well have my dreams—*to do what you can do for the wellbeing of the world and yourself, and at no harm to any humanbeing.*

They'd laid it on thick on channel 9 & it was a healing; he needed it.

3-sequential programs on Buddhism.

This sense of loss:

> Am loosing A Ho to deportation.

> Am loosing to age.

> Jasmin in my house but she must go back out, leaves me.

This forces me to seek higher things.

Amy Chung the Singing Buddhist Nun was on TV.

Those who have completely renounced this world.

Re: my work, I think it is become apparent to me there's some few people who all hang on my every word; so I will state plainly my Order—my philosophy; what is spiritual; so now it time to transcend & cement it in to some kind of movement.

It certainly is nice having a clean house.

Oh, purchased myself an on-sale shirt @ Thrift Shop—a treat for $4.20. I need this, so often run out of shirts as laundry piles and piles and piles up—even tho I wear each shirt 2 times—have now a total of 7 shirts.

Artic cold in room. No heat @ all last nite, and me fighting a cold.

Buddhist TV programs last nite—they spoke about so higher a level then the average human on this earth—its appreciating common focus, of centuries of divine prayer.

Such a ray of liberation illuminated my mind—and so many countless masses of these average people go on pilgrimages to touch this thing—what ever it is. They go to the temple to lay flowers in the stone bowls prepared by the nuns/priests—they seek this thing, which none of us can fully touch… barely knowing what it is—but how vital it is for our common sweat blood, bodily muscle existence—this finer thing!

Saturday, January 18
Walk past on street a cover; heap of blankets, underneath a jet-black face snores peacefully—mid-day.

Oh, this is what Malaysian says about new yuppie who has moved into her building—occupying a tiny room w/toilet & shower—*for $1,900:*

> Yes, she's a tekkie, a yuppie. She works in Silicon Valley. She cooks in her room—plugs in high wattage electric skillet and blows out all the fuses on the floor. The rooms aren't wired for cooking appliances —only the community kitchen. She doesn't care. She leaves her utensils in the community sink. And won't wash them for weeks. She has a tiny dog, she takes it up to the roof and walks it, it poops up there, she doesn't clean up after, the whole roof is full of dog shit. She is a mess.

A big bold FOR RENT sign; former Persian café.

Large pods of young white men walk determined this way or that down street—aggregates of tekkie workers. Software engineers.

PM
> Spirit: God has angels. You will find them very interesting Red.
> --DIFFICULT JOURNEY

Well this is how stupid I am—I got the above prophecy from Above, and did I question it? NO! Zealously wrote it down—a faithful scribe to the Almighty—then forgot it—until just re-read!

Ask to see the Angels!

Well the human conscious is certainly a strange thing—and how the forces of good act upon it. After 55-years the mysterious death of French Algerian Communist during the Battle of Algiers —freedom fighter for liberty in the nation of Algiers is solved. A French officer has confessed—he @ age of 95. His wife suddenly felt compassion for the widow of the man he had ordered to be killed and felt, unequivocally that the widow was entitled to know the truth of how & when her husband met his end. She prevailed upon her husband, the officer, and @ the age of 95, finally he gave his confession.

So sad, so horrible—persecution of My People—GLBT— in Cameroon, Africa. A very bad situation there. Murders of gay men. disrespect of TG women. The dikes have been driven into hiding. They maintain a lesbian life underground—in secret. Sexual assault, murder, beatings, intimidation. —Much of it generated by the false church purportedly of Jesus Christ— when he said to do no such thing!

Seeing one ignorant black African priest in cleric robe & collar on TV preaching miss-information he extrapolates out of our common bible. Telling lies that wound the family of humanity.

A tall beautiful black transwoman clothed in African dashiki's colorful cloth, elegantly walks thru her neighborhood, she & her grandmother are friends:

        I love my child.

Is what grandmother responds, when reporters asks if she accepts her. —The transwoman's own family has abandon her—in embarrassment, fear.

They throw away their own child in favor of gossiping haters.

They loose part of their own flesh & blood because they are so influenced by what others think.

I went out.

1963. Heat Wave. Pop hit, hit the airwaves. Flew in an airplane to New York Greenwich Village to be w/gay tribe.

Went out into the wild unknown!

Oh some counseling from OGM—

They don't want to hear that. They don't want to hear that drugs are destroying them. When you tell them that, that's why they stop coming around.

Lifted weights till 4AM.

Re: my painting; @ my best, are faces, expression. Café has not yet placed a face w/in it— nor the other 3-canvases back in kitchen drying area. Only Heart, & Time Waits For No One, in there, are done.

There are 2 kinds of instructions; the first tells you, offers you an instruction, you debate it, thinking of pros/cons w/your rudimentary thinking & then finally come into agreement w/what God has suggested. The 2nd way is God says something & you blindly accept it w/out questioning, nor meditation.

Re: coffee shop Chinese punk; this whole incident makes me think of inferiority in battle—due to being a smaller person & old, & female born (XX Chromosome) but Lord(ess) instructs this is not Her/His Way—think of the Buddha—this Buddhist show last nite—this is not the way of the monks/nuns! Theirs is the transcendental path of Peace—towards Enlightenment! It certainly is more peaceful!

Telling an artist to balance their budget is like telling a cow to saddle up in the Kentucky Derby.

In the news today you see the horrible examples of religion in charge of human affairs, of governments & their politics; anti-gay proclamations from the top of religious hierarchy which abrogates the rights of us on the bottom. –Because they cleverly dictate it thru the political process.

Lowering of standard of living for all GLBT people.

It will stop the rights of women almost immediately. This is a universal mandate for all religions who take political power—to use it to control child-baring of women—which is the future armies of nations.

Sunday, January 19

I feel like an old workhorse whose day is drawing close.

Door to a courtyard open; inside barrel chest men in red jerseys—the Great Football game party.

I had a goal to do higher things when I was a child. Higher then just support oneself sufficiently which is a decent, average, goal, but he gave all this up—security, fitting into place in society—*lets go up into the wild blue yonder* of wings, inspirational wings God gave me.

He gained the hilltop.

People wandering around the labyrinth w/puzzled looks, faces down to watch that their feet remain inside the proscribed circular lines— puzzled look seems if they want to find their way out of some mystery—which is themselves. Headed towards the center.

Saw Elaine, mentioned the news of the attempted Balmoral Hotel acquisition, razing & building a giant condo there—and she responded w/news from Detroit—the eviction of a 101-year old woman from her family home. A photo of this centurion seated outside her former house in her wheelchair, crying. Tears streamed down the old woman's wrinkled face.

The bank put her out—legally. Her son had gotten hold of her affairs, and pulled out all the $ in a series of bank loans, and spent it—on dope.

But some good-willed Samaritan heard about her over national media and went to work w/lawyers and got her put right back into her house again!

News is she just died, in her own home, age 104.

Thanks be to God!

Further, speaking of Grace not being eligible to be a historical monument—yep, she is too young! Just founded in 1929. If she ever became un-self supporting, if her waning congregations trickled down to nothing and sat there on the hilltop just a shell, a relic—w/no ongoing church services anymore, she might be sold off—torn down—this is valuable real-estate!

I equate that with the eviction of the 101-year woman from her home!

This multimillion-dollar real-estate of several hundred souls cast out into the street, or a single-family home with one aging grandmother—all the pain it brings to a congregation, or to a poor oldster.

@ the Holy Water font—Lord showed me a quick vision, a glimpse—the exit door—magnificent wood, thick, sturdy –was transformed to back door of a house w/security bars, like backdoor of a ghetto house.

The OM suddenly realized that when he went home he had nothing to do—chores—done by Jasmin—nothing to do but his work!

Sweat rolls off his back under his great green coat after climbing the hill.

Fountain gushes in the plaza, tri-color, white, red, green-blue; down the hill a great howl went up—in response to some mysterious mishap @ the football game, where the violent savages assembled.

The service was amazingly small—congregants were off celebrating the Big Game.

All the OM knew was –he was lonely.

My house shall be a house for all people—even the barefoot woman seated down the row from him, bare pink/white feet on the cold marble floor.

The OM sat there @ the outer edge of the outermost circle of the labyrinth before service—he thought: *I'm mad! I'm mad because I'm unsatisfied! How my work is not but rarely appreciated—unknown.* His work not yet done.

However the scripture proved interesting, and it's subsequent sermon, by priest Leslie Hay. Isaiah spoke; he answered God's call—but: *why have you ignored me God? Nobody knows who I am!*

78

The sermon was about Our Calling.

As said, he gazed around @ the sparse attendance, due to the football game.

The smell of Christ's Blood—wafting from the golden chalice was 100% proof alcohol.

So many are horrible, horrible, horrible; but some things are beyond even these low words—so far low—there are no words for them, but the kind of vocabulary the devils must use down in hell.

When he went out into the night air, he could feel the activity in it— simmering w/presence of so many humanbeings ordinarily not out at this time on a Sunday—but their energy was low-key.

Streets brimmed w/activity.

A small youth dressed in a red football jersey stumbled down the street he was saying: *I don't understand. I really don't understand.*

Deflated airwaves.

They had lost.

They had lost their *Big Game*.

PM
Switched on news—heard words like: *gravely disappointed*—then he knew what he had suspected.

HA HA HA! The Old Man laughed & laughed! He had prayed well! Only for one thing—peace in the city! No wild cars driving danger, bar patrons spilling destructively into the streets! That was the sole reason for his prayer! He did not hold it against them to celebrate a win, no!

The City had pulled certain busses, trains, off duty in anticipation of potential violence after the game—there has been trouble before, well-documented.

Oh! The state mailed Jasmin her first check for Home Health Care work--$1,700! She is truly happy.

> Money, fortune is not important—but what you can do with it is.
> --Countess Demitri—spoken from heaven

All the days of continuing statistics of murdered young black men; from young teens to mid-20's. Ghetto brothers. It is not these white yuppies killing each other, no.

Monday, January 20, Mt Luther King Day
Shadows begin to creep over the day.

Sat & talked w/Gary over coffee in blazing hot sun.

PM
Today is MLK Day. Let me say am glad am not living in the black/brown ghetto. As a child in a black bourgeoisie neighborhood I grew up running the neighborhood streets freely w/out harm come to me. I was light tan, others in the area ranged from dark brown to black to light tan, even white skin—of Negro ancestry. But as I grew into teenage the Civil Rights, then Pan African American movement was underway and an ugly racism reared its head inside the black community. Unknowing blacks looked @ me thinking I was white—and their virulent racism aimed @ me—fist shaking—and I was bewildered not understanding. But fortunately, simultaneously I was coming to a time of change in my life anyway—young adulthood. I realized intuitively as a 15-year old going into the night streets and neighborhood taverns to cruise for a social life, that the black South Side was not mine anymore but the artist, gay-friendly semi-integrated Near North Side, and Hyde Park could be my spots—and made my way there. As a young working adult I lived on the Near North Side where racism was not an issue—not black nor white racism. When I went out it was to these liberated beatnik-friendly taverns & cafes. When I left for San Francisco I encountered a much freer atmosphere, where again color wasn't an issue, nor gay-gender any longer. Freedom. Safety. Comfort of Place.

80

Oh! Finally got courage to open electric bill—it is not higher! The dehumidifier has done nothing.

Oh Gary & I discussed stuff and he mentioned he is house cleaning-out —like me.

He threw out a chest full of old shirts & socks. He said: *I'm purging.*

I have heard the same thing from 5 people including myself—how we are all stripping down our belongings—to be ready, to be prepared for potential removal.

Must say re: what Elaine & I spoke of last Sunday—how if Grace's congregation fell off to the point she could no longer pay her bills, and the church had to be closed down, she could be demolished & sold for fantastic realty prices. —She can't be protected as a historic monument, she isn't old enough—not yet 100 years. And thought how the church can seat 1,000, 2,000 people but the average Sunday 11AM service is but 200 or 300. Our 6-PM is 60 perhaps.

We are the skeleton which keeps this big cathedral open. We are the *remnant*, and there's a lot God can do w/that.

Tuesday, January 21
Awoke this AM to Jasmin informing me she has closed our mutual bank account—WA-MU. Well had to fiddle around w/this on phone for 15 minutes—reestablishing my other bank for Amazon direct deposit—and funds for December due to come in @ any moment! Hope it goes thru!

Now am down to just one bank. Consulted w/the Spirit before making my decision—and the fact that I would no longer have to pay $10 monthly fee must have did it.

$10 liberated towards coffee monies!

He saw the obnoxious spectacle of a pompous/officious 3rd world man in charge of glass instillation truck—into the trash-can it went.

81

The OM walked on his wei. Saw Henny @ bus stop.

Spoke to Gary of Mensa—one dear to him is in it, and mine too—
Jasmin fell 4 points short of being able to be a member when she was
a girl.

—Mensa you will recall is the global society of persons w/genius
IQ—which starts @ 185 points.

Gary theorized it led to High Expectations & if you never make
anything of your life, you are disappointed… This dilemma was
something about those eligible to be in the world's top class of brains.

Went around to the Hos in Gary's car—he off to manage his
household. Sat in sun one hour and shopped—fish fillets, and back to
standard ground beef, ugh. Spoke w/the Malaysian for some Ha Ha's.

PM
@ my age you have had a lot of victories, layered over constant
disappointment. A bedrock of continual disappointment.

Hideous world news on TV:

> 85 super rich people on this planet make the same amount of money
> as the total of 3.5 billion people –the lower classes of this earth—that
> is half the world's population.

Distribution of wealth. Karl Marx lectured about this a century ago.

The distribution of wealth in society. The 2 worst problems are:

> The abject starving poor at the societies bottom layer who are being
>   destroyed
> The hollowing out & eventual disappearance of the middle class

> ***

> Busses that PU rich yuppie tekkies are being boycotted. These
> busses that have come to symbolize the iniquities of society.
> --TV News.

82

More news about opposition against the giant shuttle busses that transport privileged tekkies to their high-wage jobs. —They can use local bus stops, while paying hardly no revenue.

Their giant corporate tekkie outfits have already moved in here, lured by promise to pay no city taxes—this is the money which goes to help the poor of our city.

> The things we produce we have absolutely no control over once we let them go.
> --TV about JD Salanger

It is a great world. It is a horrible world.

Wednesday, January 22
Eggs @ the hotel, & delicious hazelnut cookies. –Left in a sack on the lower steps beside the sidewalk.

Bus driver stops beside tall white man, also w/cane. Further away from me. –Racial typecast!

Saw one of us on bus—Henny w/cane, & mentioned Cosmo returning early from Thailand—because of the troubles there. Political unrest in the street. However he did get his share of boys.

Am glad the medical incident did not shut me out of the wonderful world completely —thru right eye—can see still a bit more clear every month after miracle shot.

> They didn't have the blueberry muffin; well those are fighting words! No blueberry muffin!
> --Shrink

The fight actually begun as no strawberry turnover!

Watched crotches jiggling past on Polk Street.

Not having a right eye to navigate with well, my depth perception is off; miss rim of glass pouring a drink.

Anticipate things are closer then they are.

Homeless. Brown gal w/her big tan belly w/yellowish stretch marks, lays out on sidewalk in the sun.

She got herself knocked up.

Its always blame the victim.

When you're a millionaire you don't really give a shit. Republicans are opposing unemployment's benefits, which have run out; bill comes up to extend it, they veto it 4 out of 5 times.

The OM found a comfy place @ Coyote near 2 men he knew, also near 2 dogs. Sunblazed bright.

Sun—just like being out @ the beach—

—Oh, the garden in the gold cauldrons has gone to hell. A green riot of fronds, stalks, & leaves shriveling & brown.

The smallish jet blax man, homeless & deranged; linty naps; wrapped up in his usual blanket shuffles by in ruined shoes that trail strings; there is no sorrow here. As he shuffles by the Spirit enlightens OM: *I'm making my way mom*—he says to his birth mother in heaven. This gentle blax soul is not what society wants to see. There is a strange reckoning on earth.

The sun is bright—blazing; the coldest winter, 1,000 miles across the continent on the other side of our country; snow blizzards 15% below zero.

It still is winter, sun high in sky will fall rapidly, disappear soon— behind the egregious rich-people condo that blocks it & shade has eaten up the pavement towards my chair.

Guess I will no longer meet Olde out here; nor see his portly body slow shuffling across the street from bus stop; jovial smile, making his way traversing the street to Coyote.

The OM stared out thru his bad eye @ traffic sign affixed on a pole down the curb; it poured into a dark pit which he couldn't comprehend.

Healing will take place.

> I was just wondering when I was going to have a good life again—
> it's a bloody hard life.
> --The Malaysian

PM
Brave blax sista-woman hero—has saved a life on freeway—2nd time she has pulled a victim out of car crash to safety!

I was given a prime directive—I knew what career I wanted, I knew it was hard, it was difficult and that most people can't do it—

TV talking about preparation to go into the work force.

Dr. Sam called—we went out to coffee, fun. However he told me a horrendous thing, which I paraphrase:

> Saw this documentary Black Fish or something, and its about a killer whale held in captivity in an amusement park, Sea World. How they lied to all the employees in Sea World, the whale has killed numerous attendants there—but they don't tell them—so these young kids go out there loving animals and wanting to help them but every so often the whale goes berserk and murders someone else—and the corporate Sea World covers it up. They tell people the killer whales in the wild only live to be 20 years old, and this whale is already 33, so they're doing it a favor, but it's a lie, the opposite is true, the whale is 20 and the in the wild they can live up to 35. Its amazing how they trap the whales for captivity. They spot a whale pod and go after them—the whales are intelligent, they might be smarter then humans. They all dive under the ocean, then the males head up to surface and out towards the shore and at first the humans would speed after them, thinking the whole pod was going there, but the females & their pups dive down deeper & go off by a secret route—but eventually cunning humans figured this out, and this killer whale was captured as a pup. He has been raised in the amusement park and has fathered practically all the

killer whales in captivity—but not like you think, no, his sperm is harvested to artificially inseminate the cows, so he doesn't even get to visit lady whales. The point of the picture asks the question should wild animals ever be held in captivity for any reason other then to actually preserve their species, I think not!

Dear God, I pray for this whale held in captivity, let my cry come unto Thee.

Sam's theory; see what happens to short men—they are picked on from childhood, they are bullied; it scars them for life; they grow up w/that training. But we didn't grow up w/that training because we grew up as women.

We react to bullies surprisingly different then a regular man who has been trained to submit, so we shock them when we speak out, when we stand up.

TV program on how typhoon Hyian decimated Philippines—must say the scene of the town in the TV footage, dirt, unpaved roads teaming w/swarms of so many young children was obnoxious. A previous documentary reported the average family there has 20 children. Poor families have child after child—all in a state of poverty. The working father cannot afford to feed more then 6 or 7 children—he is incapable of working more then 80-hours a week, beyond any human limit. But they will not use birth-planning. 1st point; only this year has the government finally overturned legislation which prevented *discussion* of birth control for half a century. 2nd, Philippino men do not want to use protective measures —rubbers— which they claim interferes w/sexual pleasure. Which threatens their masculinity. Centuries ago when the Philippine natives had not yet been invaded by foreigners, their midwives and wise women had native techniques to reduce birth rate. The takeover of their island by the Catholic Church has altered this balance. European invention has changed their island to swarms of impoverished children—for some interest of the Church's own.

Thursday, January 23
Down here & heard folks just left. Have 2 cans C-food which must be carried back home.

Sit in sun.

Great time last nite w/Doctor friend.

Sun hot but feel a breeze coming on, unperceivable, heralding the late afternoon cool.

OH! MOW, Meals On Wheels delivered me a heater! Small plug-in heater for those wretched cold nites the boiler in basement is not functioning. So far this dehumidifier hasn't run up my bill so a heater might not either.

The OM felt no one was going to show up & that the causal friends he was forming might not go further. He was going to be lonely a bit & thought of his option—Evensong @ the pinnacle of the hill @ the cathedral, but thought: *no, its too lonely. Everyone disappears afterwards. They probably all go off w/friends to dine elsewhere.*

The OM sat in the sun no one he really knew was out other then the lady who had inadvertently been involved in that huge brouhaha between him & the Hawk & the wan young man in wheel chair so long ago...

Well as you know we are all here engaged in a struggle to survive, probably much less live well—so it, the struggle to earn bread & board, is a preoccupation really from doing other things—reaching out more thoroughly to find friendship for instance.

Sweat was rolling down under his grey & black checked shirt—no one was out—still he could see the figure of Olde Jolly w/sparse white hair & cane only in a dream.

Well – as you well know—the people come & people go, passing to/fro Coyote; poor men in bluejeans washed to fade, grey gymshoes of the poor; who carry the inevitable backpack... Grey beard of the old poor; & women w/their satchels packed full of belongings looking even worse—our lives could be better.

Mood music plays directly out of Coyote loud speakers.

—It would be fun & he could fantasize many things—but long after w/nothing to do but go home—it seems our ever challenged life is reduced to just the gruel Oliver Twist was denied & what we do have is just to keep us going on one foot-fall after another, living another day—

Deep music grinds on like church, sonorous, hinting @ great mysteries @ space travel & future yet to unfold. And solutions, requiring great risk.

Now shade devoured the parklet & he was glad he'd chosen this place having set here before, one w/optimum sun where sun stayed the longest to warm him.

I see the disappointed faces.

Am in the Hos. All of the regulars are still up @ the church @ seniors.

Sun.

I have purchased 2 packages of beef for Jasmin to take home & cook for me.

We must give thanks for in what God has placed us.

The OM was agitated; he didn't know why. He prayed it was not a premonition of some kind of major shootout in the TL for instance—every so often Jasmin would call him:

> Where are you!
>
> Out @ the coffee shop.
>
> Well go home & don't go out!
>
> What!

There's a crazed man loose in the Tenderloin he's shot 6 people they're dead! They're looking for him now! It's on the news! Go home & stay there!

What!

Go home! & stay home!

Sat in Ho's bench in sun warming; felt himself vaguely wanting to curl up in fetal position & drift out of conscious.

Generous is key word today. —World is so fucked up, being human seems that we short-change each other for profit—result is people are always short of cash so they have to steal, dip their fingers in the pot, chisel, to make up for it.

He question the Lord(ess) what to do.

What do you want me to do today?

PM
Many people don't want a state of living out their entire lives being either awake or asleep. Many seek the recreational zone—of being high, on alcohol, painkillers, marijuana, or herbs.

News from Middle East—tribal elders order gang rape of 28-year old woman as punishment for some offense.

Well I have spent so much of my thoughts & subsequent writing on trying to make sense of the world—to give a logical skeleton to it's weighty human mess, its injustice; & have won many wars on the invisible battlefield of thought & analysis; of discourse, discussion & rant. –Inside my own head. My only solace is that much of the world is starting to agree w/me. We have arrived @ these thoughts of justice together.

Now to see it done would be splendid.

Suddenly occurs to me my life has all fallen into place. My money, services, living-space, talents. Have only now to live out the remainder of my life creating as much more fine arts paintings & writings as possible!

News. Flames are spreading over some major cities of the world— Kiev, Bangkok, Cairo, Syria; will it spread all over the planet?

Terror. Raw terror. Small factions lashing out at each other; @ everyone else.

Hell come up from the pit.

Friday, January 24
L. has purchased Jasmin a car! Her own car!

Native American Dental clinic; Indian educational TV; thoughts on suicide —tell yourself to keep holding on to what things you like to do—that is a reason to live.

I got to go down to the gutter to get real shit; to find out the truth.

Here where I always sit waiting for my dentist, watching Native American education TV channel. Which is full of holistic facts for living—especially for poor folk.

Sit here in dentist chair blax music jams, am high as a kite on meds.

PM
A w/brother Baz briefly was able to pay him back $60 of the remaining $80 I owe him thru cash & food w/food stamps. Am so glad to have lowered down all these people. My budget is clearing up!

Fun w/brother Baz, if just for a brief minute. Spoke T language— which one cannot do w/just everybody:

> There is seminar tomorrow about bottom surgery.

> Phallo or medio?

> Both.

Show & tell? Or just talk?

Think some guys are going to show their new dicks.

Dr. XX was trained in Serivio.

That's the place all the best FTM surgery is coming from these days.

Would you have phallo?

I'd rather not think about it. Just have to make do w/what I've got. Too many guys have gotten messed up.

The operations not perfect yet.

Not sure if there is sensation—they can't guarantee it will feel as good as it did before.

And guys lie so much; if a guy lost sensation in getting a dick, he might not admit it. He might not admit it because he's lying to himself—much less lying to any of us.

So he's got a dick—just to stand & pee, and to pack his trousers—but no sex!

Saturday, January 25
Greet Junior & Gary around @ Coyote; bought the lad w/food stamps:

> Ice cream
> Strawberry milk
> Chocolate moon pie

Younger straight white men bellow loudly about men raping a man in sci-fi movie: *Hold Him Down!*

Fuck him up the ass!

Big shouting match @ Coyote Singing Man & Woman With Dog #1, and me. On the subject of transsexual bathrooms no less! Something the Singing Man knows little about, but he shouts in a loud voice anyway—most unpleasant.

Shouting match Singing Man, Woman W/Dog about transsexual bathrooms continues far too long—and in a high decibel.

'Grims to piss & purchase some small item as tribute, like an oceania roll (toilet paper) —then to Hos.

In the infernal Ho's grocery-basket line.

Hope to hear from brother Baz tonight. Jasmin tomorrow.

Comancho from BABYLON FALLING called from New York. & hee-hawed out on Ho's park bench uproariously, loud. He was undergoing horrible weather. Snow, ice, —10 below zero.

Al Goldstein has died, founder of Screw Magazine, which did a brief 2 column review of LUCY & MICKEY. (Circa 1996.) He died in ignominy & poverty. In one of his last interviews w/Comancho Goldstein said: *all the people I knew betrayed me & stole my money.* In the New York Times obits these same men are photo'd clustered around his bedside like they were dear old friend—but this seems not to be the case.

Told Comancho all the neighborhood gossip, about who is dead, whose shop has been sold, and etcetera.

He & wife Kensey & dog Lou, are undergoing horrible East Coast weather. Cold, ice, blizzards.

Never before seen in this town—large groups of young well dressed men, w/2 women among them packs of 8 to 15—teckies—on their wei to dine. Horrible co-workers of an Internet pod.

Huge amount of white men w/Asian women couples. Of course the white men/white women couples—but where are the left-out Asian men?

Was on phone a long while on Ho's bench.

Shadows have fallen into dark pretty lights red, blue, green; pronounced music spills out of taverns.

PM
300 years of colonialism, 20 years of democracy; in South Africa— 80% of white South Africans are rich, 80% of black South Africans are poor. Go figure.

One of the most difficult things in a transsexual life is puberty. West Side Story—the tale of pubescent youth gangs involved in turf wars. Immediately in the picture a butch dike is kicked out of the gang—it is male-born only. There are no effeminate men.

These street gangs have no place for queers.

Thus, effectively, we are all written out of the motion picture just as it begins. Also, no women in the gangs, only adjuncts, for their boys love life.

Of course in NYC, and in SF we created gangs of our own.

We were a street scene, milling about, funning.

I guess up in heaven would be all the good things I didn't have on earth.

Green scratching AREEEEEKKKK!!!!

Finally got online this PM, went to Amazon to take down my old DOING IT FOR THE MISTRESS, and STREET OF DREAMS—and entered in the new Text POD edition of both. So much easier to process! Just have books on hand so when get a sale, I must send these, and restock myself thru ordering again from POD.

Gone is finding master copy taking to photocopy to run out an edition, bring home, cut pages in half, paginate them, punch holes in them & put thru spine, then wrap up, then go to Post Office, stand in line, to mail out.

Sunday, January 26

Feel horrible—abused myself w/chocolates last nite & temporarily put on 4 pounds. Feel bad. Help me God(ess).

Just heard a horror up heah' cathedral—another is dismissed; discontinued; head rolling.

Out on the plaza Muslims take photos of each other w/large camera, gear in this holy place—as it should be.

The OM sat; he waited to receive what he was to read for a scripture, as Lector 1. He sat looking out of his 1.5 eyes thinking how well suited he was to receive the fun he desired. The sex, fun, laughs, jollies, & food! & praise! He was a mess.

He knew he was being tortured by the Eternal God.

He sat in the Cathedral's front beside the indoor labyrinth. Gazed upward. The gay streamers looked like a waterfall. Appeared to be as if its raining—red, blue, streamers—a thousand shimmering strands.

> What would you do?
>
> I would serve God the Lord(ess).
>
> —In His/Her way?
>
> You want me to serve You, yes. In Your way.

Again the Savior was calling.

All the things you fancied to do for God.

It might not be the things you fancied you'd do, but other things.

TM walked to the podium, which was miked. As Lector 1, he read the scripture—one of Paul (ugh)'s letters to a church speaking of their disagreements—and how a church might want to kick a certain person out for an offense, then someone else might want to kick a different

94

person out for some other offense—well after it was all said & done, there'd be no church left!

But we would be fragmented, driven apart. No one would be left. And not one stone of the temple left standing upon another.

God, I was so nervous & self-conscious in my school days, the ruling kids @ school were white & more sophisticated; I had my own black/brown crowd in which I was fully a member—but in the highschool pageants, class room dynamics, we were defiantly outcasts. All of us black-brown, tan, were automatically rendered 2nd class. Also, in the bar life—I was awkward, shy & poor! As in the literary life, not part of any inner circle—who published themselves over & over again faithfully. I was accepted into street life.

The OM noticed how the congregation was positioned; the 3 silent unacknowledged transsexuals positioned apart; 2 of us in front, me on one side, an MTF on the other— unplanned; my silent brother in the back.

3 garbage cans in front of hotel next door been torn apart in a frenzy. A hungry homeless, who is enraged.

One by one the named months fly past, never to return—this is how time goes, it is finite; it does not repeat. We await God, the Infinite.

PM
Tunisia! Passed its democratic constitution! One of the few middle-eastern nations w/a democratic constitution not based on Islamic law! Which guarantees gender equality! Viva Tunisia!

Freedom of speech, equality between men & women.

Monday, January 27
No one here. —Yet.

In a brief while the OM spied young Junior walking directly down Polk Strassa w/a bedroll of a glaring, unmistakable orange/red color, so that it could not be missed—signaling that the youth was part of the army of homeless.

He stands, lounging against the cement wall of Coyote Café —his predatory pose—prepared to ask passerby's for a cigarette.

We talk only briefly, then he departs.

A demented Asian talks loudly to himself; gesticulates artistically. Soon TM saw him exit the Hos w/2 free coffees, one in each hand.

@ Ho's; bought 3 packages of beef for Jasmin to cook for me—so excellently, as she did the others.

When we get a certain age—we get the message. We are all going to die. This lays at the end of our voyage.

PM
The keeper of the mores of civilization has long been the church.

It amazes me to think that people cannot believe that all human flesh is still human—no matter our high positions, nor great deeds. The priests, bishops, cardinals, of a religious place, the Imams, priests and hierarchy of a great mosque, the nuns, priests, & rank and file deacons, ushers, chairman's of the board—not to mention presidents of great universities of acclaim and longevity—to know that people endow them w/super powers as to their morality, correct-thinking, and will not attribute to them any human flaw or shortcoming, will not allow it, can't stand to hear of it—oh how disappointed they will be! –When they found out this bitter truth!

They will fall to the ground gnashing teeth—if those they elected are indicated in scandal. They will weep bitter tears while tearing up their pledge cheques, they will go into hiding for embarrassment when those they endorse fall flaming to the ground from their pedestals, breaking apart in the dirt; they will leave town, they will abdicate the church taking their children w/them and their helpless old people in wheelchairs—wheeling them as far and as fast as they can to get away from the now-stained, and tarnished church—the violated institution—whose days of truth have emerged!

La scandalè!

To think that we are not human—not subject to all the rises and falls of nature, bad moods, pain, angst, desire, —just because we hold a Doctor of Divinity, or some other degree—that human flesh has concocted!

To get across to them a point I want to make—some of these disillusioned people actually believe because of the above *human* shortcomings—of those priests & powerful leaders of the church— that there is no God! This of course is the bad part of it all.

If you ever tell any of them anything—tell them this! Red Jordan, tell them this!

It was this very thing which had turned young transboy away from the love of God, from the embrace of our Savior Jesus Christ—@ a very young age. *The hypocrisy of the church.* The hypocrisy of those who claimed Christianity, yet acted unfeeling & blind towards his predicament of abuse—within his middle-class bourgeoisie home.

Know the difference—

Red Jordan Arobateau
Tuesday, February 4, 2014
3:30 AM, Pacific Standard Time
San Francisco, CA

Part- 3

Turkey, Ukraine, Greece are trying to turn towards the West, which currently is the European model—and away from the old Eastern regimes. They want European Union standards—which means maximum freedom, female/male equality, gay rights, separation of church & state.

Oh! Ukraine riots have spread out of Kiev—the capitol, to all the cities of that nation! This thing is now too big to be contained! The old order must step down! The young protesters claim they are going to hold elections and elect themselves to power! Hopefully it will not be as corrupt as the old guard. Hopefully they will gain admittance to the EU and abide by those principals, —which make a more democratic, equalitarian society!

> *There is another world.*

> —Another world beyond this?

> *Yes.*

Oh wow! MOW to come over tomorrow 9am and deliver me a new flat screen TV, and install it! Free! WOW to MOW!

Next, Jasmin to come over w/sacks of laundry! YEAH! Clean fresh laundry!

Oh Junior and I spoke about him going to City College & try to get some schooling. If I could let him stay @ my place. I said we'd have to go thru a lot of steps first. The first one being dedicating himself to keeping a cellphone, and not treating it so casually as he treated them before. (Selling them off for dope, cash, food.)

Now am worried about me telling him this, because if he drives me crazy and I can't stand it, and have to throw him out, this won't help him any either, to be again disappointed, much less by me, so it could turn into a situation where we both loose.

We must make rules I can live by and that he can actually do!

Tuesday, January 28

Things will be taken from you—things will be added to you.

MOW came by this AM –TV. Bright, young, helpful Philippino—he assembled the set & programmed it in.

Next Jasmin over w/vacuum cleaner, vacuumed floor & cleaned birdcage—Bijou's—& brought me a coffee in a bottle—leftover from L's breakfast; thanks Be To God!

Sun blazing hot—no OGM's.

Well it is always the crippled pigeon who lingers around the longest, who approaches closer.

The Old Man could often be found w/pigeons beside his feet; maybe these had come to learn to trust those big boots would not stomp @ them.

A stupid man of color ran, took a flying leap feet first and came down to stomp on the flock of pigeons—he was a fool! For they wildly flew off even before his feet left the sidewalk.

Justice! Justice! I'm a God of justice—take it seriously!

God is heavy duty!

Cosmo drove by w/a car full of boys—we are back to normal.

Reggae music today.

Leather clad motorcycle men pull their iron horses up to curb into parking zone; like days of the hitching post of the Wild West.

Destiny.

All the young people inside on Internet, bent studiously over their tables—only OM set outside, looking outward, cruising the street— for trade. Males. For friends made.

A white car drives by, honks, OGM's inside wave. Nun stopped & Junior has not showed.

So I'm on my wei.

Got letters of fear in mail. One from Social Security. The other from property management.

I think a lot of people are very afraid—of having their $ taken from them.

The Lord(ess) comforted the OM, saying: *its nothing to worry about.*

Sure enough he relaxed his tense shoulders—his eyes squinted in protective fear widened back into the normal gaze of a humanbeing busy w/tasks.

He opened the letters after awhile—both were to his advantage.

The Social Security was just an earning report of the year as a tax statement. And the letter from the property management gave his yearly rent board refund—a low $5.15 this bleak year—and announcement of the annual rent raising this coming March—not $20 of the last several years but a mere $10! So his rent had not yet risen to $1,100! Being in total, for still another year, a few dollars less.

PM

> This is a real revolution. A revolution of the people—
> --TV lady observer; Ukraine

TM was a jolly king. A king in his own domain.

There are many who are kings—you see them on TV large as kings— but they shouldn't be kings—not really are of a kingly material.

They are self-concocted, bought & paid for, airbrushed, shams.

On news, 1,000-mile long storm hits our Deep South.

What's truly bothersome is its 60 degrees one day, then the next its 8 above zero…
--Megan Wolfe, now in Ole' Miss

Wednesday, January 29

I see another stupid yuppie sto' gone out of biz—butcher-block paper in the windows obscuring view of clean up, move out—Bacchus De Silvia—now gone. It featured slim young white European models flavored rich.

Saw blind man on bus w/older German shepherd. His way is difficult. He taps w/cane across fast-moving intersection.

Moments later, large black van calmly drives thru red light across Van Ness intersection. Loud horn honks of disapproval.

See how much of our universe depends on blind faith.

Rain in the air. Gulls shriek ERRRKKKK! They are dealing w/the yuppie rich invasion, they fly high overhead, and roost in the eves of tall buildings far away from the maddening throng.

Just left Shrink.

Gave me instructions how to handle Junior. Knowledge to hook him up to Dimensions Youth Shelter.

Am @ Coyote—seated inside by door w/view outside.

Cold air blows in door around my ankles. Stream of customers comes & goes.

It's a cold day. Miserable.

Insistence of dew—not rain—yet every little bit helps.

Called Megan (*—Megan Wolfe, artist-photographer/writer) from Coyote. She told me the brief tale of various people she's been encountering down home in Holly Springs—who have just abdicated San Francisco, or other big cities because they can no longer manage their astronomical rent:

102

They're miserable being back down here. Especially if you're a performing artist. You need an audience. You need a venue. Its not quite as bad for a writer, a photographer, an artist—you can communicate on the Internet; sell your stuff online, and send out material from your home base –to galleries, publishers, but you can't do your live performance except w/a live audience.

After two attempts to get Blax art gallery to see my stuff—gong thru 2 young white curators, on wei downtown, passed by the lady's gallery—a striking photo hung in its window from 1940's that made me stop: *Colored Only* sign. How disparaging. To have lived under the oppression of those times, as did my grandmother, grandfather, & those before them.

As I stood outside musing on the memorial photo, who did I see but a lady who seemed to be the owner herself, brown, slender, well-dressed & in command—so I waited, as it seemed she was approaching the door. When she came out I asked was she the gallery owner, she said yes, I said: I'm Red Jordan Arobateau and she extended her hand, we shook hands:

I'm an artist of color and I wonder if you'd like to see my slides—I've got them on my flashdrive.

Handed her my biz card with an oil from1970 on it. She said she'd look me up and we parted ways.

So there! Fate had it that I would accomplish my goal—first gallery owner to look @ my stuff— (Lost Dog; circa 1969 Oil on Canvas 36" x 20") at least!

Near Grant Writing Center talk w/XX, blax man who plays accordion for coins:

How are you?

Worried.

Oh what's wrong?

I'm worried until my SSI check comes in. I worry until I get it in my hands, so I can pay my room rent. It's due in 3 days.

Oh, yeah, I know the feeling. Its hard to do your art when you worried about money.

How true this was. So many times in the confusion of life he had not strength to do his God-appointed tasks, due to fear. Abject fear of a loss of even the few coins that kept his ship afloat, that an affluent person would not blink at, nor those living in a truly compassionate— and *effectively managed*—society would be.

A younger man stares up @ me—a man, yet traces of woman. I heard his voice across the room and had come over to investigate:

Hi, do I know you?

Yes hello, I know you.

I'm Red.

I'm XX.

Here we two are, in the library. Two transsexual souls. From his desk he looks up, solemn, grey-blue eyes; we probably saw each other @ one of the many meetings, conferences, for Our Kind, a glimpse of these men-women etched in each others retina, into our brain.

PM
Pete Seger died. Folk singer. Group—the Weavers. Communist. Fighter for justice in America & the world. –In New York City.

About The Weavers—this socialist-leaning folksinging group takes its name from the original weavers—one of the early trade unionists from the 12th century in pre-industrial England.

The weavers had been once a proud cottage industry. Each family took home work—bought materials, and spun @ home for a living, utilizing husband, wife, and all children old enough to do some part of the process. They were able to command a good wage, have a house, buy furniture, food, a cow, & some chickens. Eat meat.

A new application came into the garment weaving industry, in the 18th century, the mechanical loom. —Which people heralded as modern, efficient, and a benefit for humankind! Simplifying the tasks of workers. Problem was—it reduced the once-proud weavers to slaves in their industry—cutting their wages to the bone. Left them in starvation—selling off the furniture in their house for bread so as not a 3-legged stool was left to sit on, and they had to squat in the dirt and lay to sleep on blankets.

The Industrial Revolution brought starvation to countless.

One must always consider the opposite side of the coin.

The OM sat writing his picayune NOTES—one eye on the page, another on the street, which paraded on foot past the wide-opened doors of Coyote. Now he saw umbrellas—oh, he was lonesome.

OH! Just spoke w/Jasmin! She is paying for me an Internet access in my studio!

YEAH!!!!!!

Well I'll tell you, compassion is the extra accelerating force that drives help to extend to poorer hands & justice to rain down, but finally if people would just obey the laws—the human race would be allright!

It does not take this Herculean attempt by all! This extraordinary expansion of energy. – Just do the simple Golden Rule & that's that!

Love God w/all your heart. Love your neighbor as yourself!

Thursday, January 30
This is a ruthless city—no place for Jasmin, my care worker to park, so she must drive off. Thought the OM sourly; he walked down his long hall, lonely, not graced by the presence of his former wife & friend—a lonely old man—but moments later his phone rang again

heralding the MOW delivery— blax lady informed him that Jasmin can get something called Meter Card Parking & permit from the city—and park free in the delivery zone right outside! This would be fabulous—especially seeing it's always empty since there is not a lot of deliveries to businesses, thus it is not cluttered up by ordinary cars! Har!

Foul smell rising out into the wind after passing by homeless man laying in filth & rags on the cold concrete sidewalk.

A crowd of pigeons feasted, round heads together in a cluster, beaks pointed down, pecking, which elevated their tails up in air in a circular fan—dining, after TM had gone past dropping several slices of rye crisp & smashing them gently w/his boot—crushing them down to bird-size portions.

The Lord/ess has been talking to me a lot these recent days—S/He'd throw me a rope to hang on to, to move me about from one place to another where I desired to go more easily.

Well the killing part is that we are discriminated against in an unconscious fashion. –People judge us, simply not aware of what they are doing.

> The young ones are kinder, hopeful; the old ones, they've already been beaten up by social conditions so many times –that's why they're mean.
> --Wisdom from the Malaysian

Sun is finally out.

He sat outside the magnificent place—in its inner courtyard. Above, the belltower, stark, a rampart; graystone, against bleu/white cloud-moving sky; their planet earth was twirling & moving around the sun @ a fast clip—*is it what made the sky drift so fast?* He mused

> Look! Look! There's the bell tower! And this part that they built after the 60's. All these buildings—where they give events.
> --Tourist, to child

106

We are headed towards the alter—God's alter. One comes in blind, led by a dog & tapping w/a cane; another half-blind; another one on crutches of old age, another in a wheelchair.

Another holds hands w/a blax mentally ill.

Here we assemble w/all our infirmities.

Great Evensong—Instillation of two new priests.

@ service tonite was heard to TM (via the Spirit) some Good News—about this church—Grace Cathedral being a place to go on towards God, towards Paradise, this place being a boulevard connecting us to the Divine. Any church you select—or that selects you—is your boulevard.

PM
However the dirty gossip heard is that 6—yes 6 more people are leaving us! Some are being let go. Others retiring. Others taking up new callings. You see it is the spectrum of bad to nostalgic.

Syrian president is an abnormal freak. He has a weird body type, extra tall and a strange face. He might be a mentally damaged, or spiritually undone soul. He has sent out bulldozers thru his nation demolishing whole areas who voted for his rival candidate. 200 hectares, buildings from 1 or 2 stories to eight stories high, reduced to rubble; thousands of citizens displaced, now homeless.

Friday, January 31
Am in sun @ Coyote –Liza (Woman W/Dog #1) & Gary—talked:

> Red: My Shrink told me I shouldn't let Junior stay @ my house—I don't need the stress.

> Liza: It would be a mistake. Their brains haven't grown & then, there's the drugs—they don't have boundaries. Tell them they can't use your computer, leave them alone, the first thing they do—get on your computer and something's broken.

Am now in Ho's bench in sun—*Da!* Seated next to Rooski woman on cellphone, yelling animatedly *Da! Da!* like a Russian peasant.

Oh! Now I find out the Church founded in 1849! So she is definitely a landmark heritage and the City will not allow her to be tore down!

Grace chapel. First a small church, then a large church—that burnt down in earthquake & fire of 1906. Then moved on to it's replacement where we are today.

By now I had seen far too many examples of people who do chose the wrong path, they chose to go the wrong way. Really chose it. Chiefly among the mentally ill & those addicted to drugs or alcohol.

Its very cold. Head cold. Might have to bring warm Roosky hat out tomorrow.

Was told that the Singing Man went & purchased my Junior a slice of pizza—of course the bells of jealousy ring w/in me—which is ridiculous. Am not jealous of any of the other OGM Junior has had sex w/for money. Plus don't really know if this is an act of kindness, or one of backstabbing me!

PM
Last nite @ reception one of the chalice bearers/servers said they had a person who came up, took the communion, then spit it out on the alter.

Of course we can understand this—those deeply wounded by religion. Those destroyed in God's Name.

Assembled the tools of masturbation.

Ah! Har!

Many transsexual women were once highly placed males—big, strong, intelligent, loved by their families, respected by their community in which they were growing up—until they manifested the first signs of effeminacy—then they fell from grace & became despised. Throughout their lives following they have an agenda, a struggle; they have to regain that status again—except as women.

No wonder they are so obnoxiously competitive; no wonder they keep on using male strategies so well—one that worked for them in their previous lives.

Well you must know that you are just madly creating—for decades an artist's mind may be in a state of confusion—as how to market themselves, what to do about finances; this & that, and they are playing a hopscotch game, leaping from rock to rock in the onrushing onslaught of life—madly creating, wildly envisioning & committing that vision to paper, to canvas, to the boards; it is finally in old age they get a grip on themselves—realizing they have no money, no security.

Blax sister in Ho's lot said to me:

> You are blessed to live to such an old age. Many, many, do not live to be an old age—they die young, you are very privileged to live so long, you are highly favored!
> --L., Christian woman

People are born into racial groups, they identify by gender & type, and form communities around this, but sometimes they destroy their communities; drive each other out into isolation, into suicide; they cut, cut & cut their own numbers until they cut their numbers to pieces; they are rendered ineffective—as a group power.

Saturday, February 1
The OM was thinking nasty thoughts—that was what kept him going down these streets. Nasty thoughts about naked males! Strong hairy chests & turgid dicks. Naked females w/hot pungent cunts & big titties jugging!

> All right dude! Go write your depressing novels!
> --Young Man Alex

Are my novels depressing?

Do you know how many steps you have left to take on this earth how many breaths left to draw? No you don't—& each is precious.

Therapist warns me actively not to take Junior home anymore. Stress might kill me!

We all must go, even Olde Jolly.

Age 92, still, heart pumping.

Blax man ½ naked walks down middle of street flowing w/vehicles waving his hands; in a delusion he is trying to direct it like a traffic officer.

See the ugly spirited Hawk; her wonderful big poodle close & also holding tightly his/her purse—recall the purse's name was Esther or some such.

Of interest, the Malaysian's friend, white guy, told us he saw a man being arrested on California Avenue—for yelling. He was yelling top of his lungs, an Asian officer came out tells him: *put you hands up against the wall, put them behind your head,* he cuffed him and put him in the patrol car—he might release him in the TL. Or he might take him in and book him—he'll be out the next day.

Corner liquor store, long vacant encased in new plywood, being remolded. Serviced by Latino workmen. What yuppie horror is going to appear there?

Streets are yuppie—busy.

Bustling, settling in for tomorrow's big game.

So what is the type, caliber of a person?

Our lives will prove this as it plays out.

> You think about the past, good times; you can't go back! All you can do is sit back & cry.
> --The Malaysian

Her friend, the white man told OM his scheme to dry clothes—wash out in sink, then put clothes in microwave to dry them!

Socks!

He looked around for the bond-pigeon but it didn't return again that day.

PM
Hot-bodied birds pushing out heat on my neck. Green, white.

Sunday, February 2
If you talk about 1 song that led us out here—2,000 miles from home to an unknown place it was California Dreamin' —played over & over on national airwaves—the star pop hit of 1963.

Had a lot of trash to place in his trashcan as he approached the Cross @ the asp. As the OM came forth towards the golden Cross & its delta in marble on the upper stair—he saw a tourist—snapping— w/their camera. Later when he approached the candle stand, people w/children milled around.

The light is burning.

The lost & bewildered come here.

Great gothic cathedral.

One newcomer, a Caucasian man asked a woman of color beside him:

> How come you're not home watching the Super bowl?

> The Super bowl—what is she?

I bow to the Eternal God.

Her great gothic arches; her turrets & towers—her high inspiration.

The woman who was always so greatly bored let out a deep loud sigh; groans of supreme boredom.

We are all here.

The OM gazed round over far reaches of the cathedral, across the labyrinth's huge circumference set down in white marble.

Parishioners stood on there in their places like chess pieces.

The vibraphone, sonorous.

The pageant begins.

Deep groans—*oh Gawd.... Ahhhuhhhhh....*

Streamers, blue & red; breaking up light w/shadow.

The streamers still hung down from 8 story rafters above, each 100 feet long, moving w/currents of air; by shadow & light transformed the middle aisle of white granite so that it stretched to a shimmering river extended from the Cross to the entrance in front and out into the street by indication, some 1,200 feet.

Priest Jude prayed for all the church, for all not in the church, for all who have been harmed and injured by the church in the past. And OM was sure the bored woman was one of those harmed—later, bored or not, she honored the Body and Blood of Jesus by taking the communion.

One in attendance, suspiciously like a hater, sent up a frightening prayer which lasted a very long time—condemning the wickedness that can be found in the City of San Francisco, which, they seem to believe has seduced their child. It cast a condemnation on all that heard it, and were hyper weary, such as Transman who did not need any condemnation whatsoever, being already a pre-weakened person.

It is sincere. His seeking of the Eternal, his worship, no matter his horrible moods.

Lord of justice.

Ohh... (Loud moans.) Service is about to end!

PM

I'm so tired and it's so hard trying to go thru your life, trying to make sense out of all these missing pieces.

Prescription needles wrong again. The size of my prescription syringes has been gotten wrong for 3 years.

Black, white, tan, skin. Naked bodies that were once souls—now lost to the insanity of drugs.

The rises & falls of fate. Just as you are going up one path, another opens up, not as good in some ways, better in others, and you are pushed off in a new direction.

The OM's food card given to him from Grace this month was @ the Ho's—which was far simpler—being his regular shopping store, but the miscellaneous household products he had begun to purchase w/it were far more expensive @ the low-down Ho's compared to the Safeway store:

> Toilet paper
> Dish detergent
> Laundry detergent
> Dental floss

Monday, February 3
Self-cocooned under blankets laying out on sidewalk, his/her walker standing alone some 7 steps away; a few articles of clothing shed inbetween. Despondent. Homeless. Has given up.

Thank God the comforting sun is here. I'm baking.

It is a mad dance, a whirlwind. Must get doctor on phone to sign paper for parking for my health care worker; it makes life so difficult all these entanglements which take time to straighten out.

Well God is like a steamroller life presses on, no matter what—thru all hang-ups. Crazy human machinations.

Seated in the parklet; here is the inevitable big loud man; making you uneasy; remember, you have rights—they are held to the same constraints as you—by our society.

Brushes, ink pens, produced stealthily from a satchel; a graffiti artist crouches beside a wall—*the wall is my canvas*.

A bare surface. Vacant, plain, faded color; embellished w/barest of geometric designs—a tempting sight—because it is blank.

When you grow up colored, Negro, blax, African-American, you get to know some traits of your people by heart—for instance knuckle cracken' —seems a lot of the folks crack their finger joint. Look over here a bone-cracken' blood, jes' pulling on they fingers.

PM
Well as have said—poor San Franciscans are stuck in a holding pattern living in the same dreary units, looking in the faces of those we don't particularly like forever—because we cannot change. We cannot move. We don't have enough money to pay the new high rents. Our rent control units have become a jail. A security. A safety net. But confining. Definitely not the freedom most citizens had 20 years ago to move from one part of town to another. —To a different street, a fresh unit!

Tuesday, February 4
Comancho called—wants to do a photo-interview w/Shaun Roberts of me, in my studio. To put up on his website online.

Heavy yellow painted earth-moving machines, gouge out great bites of old Jack Tar Hotel on Van Ness Ave; towering 15 floor relic of cement/rebar. Elbow of the gargantuan crane bent @ 5th story— ripping out walls; makes way for the installation of a new private hospital—for the rich. Money can buy their health services.

The crane's companion, a small busy yellow earthmover runs on its treads over pile of rubble—1 story thick high broken cement fragments—eating up mouthfuls to shovel into waiting dump trucks that await in a revolving procession.

The foul air—all cough as they past by —from dust kicked up, this powder of destroyed cement. Workman stands upon the mountainous rubble & hoses it down w/streams of white water.

They stare @ me when they think I'm not looking & they turn away—decries a mean street kid, scared; white pale skin, flaming red blond hair as red as my name, he throws a mock punch @ blax street kid homie in jest.

Talked to T (OGM) about politics, and he lambastes one we know, the Singing Man:

> Enormous crazy thing about him is he is a Republican & he's poor! He sides w/everything they do! No stranger thing then a poor Republican! Being $ money is who the Republicans are all about!

Cosmo walks by w/3boys in tow, going to eat. He calls out a fleeting *hello*.

Gathered @ the Ho's benches in brief confab w/The Malaysian & Dennis. We spoke of the impending doom rolling thru this city catching who it may—of renters evictions, condo conversations, owner-move in's—and all 3 of us agreed we had an eagle eye out for other cheep places we might flee to if times hit us that slaughterhouse punch. The Malaysian captured the moment:

> I told the owner I want to die here. I want to die here, right in my place.

PM

> You got to walk that lonesome valley.
> You got to walk it for yourself.
> Ain't nobody else kin' walk it for you.
> You got to walk it all alone.

An old Hillbilly song, its harsh, it's real.

Its symbolic references are to this life and this world—as it passes, and us in it. This song spoke to the bare existence those tough survivors endured.

115

The story of Ann Bolyin—2nd wife of the tyrant Henry the VIII—of legend—we do not know if she was innocent or guilty of treason to the Crown.

There are no eyewitnesses to the events—which happened in the 1500rds, some 500 years ago. There were records of court proceedings, letters, diaries—written down w/pen & ink, some of which survive, a lot are missing leaving vacant gaps in the account. Oral tradition for court gossip didn't exist. No one was passing the horrendous tale down by word of mouth faithfully for generation after generation. So we have had to piece together what happened—unless some new documents surface—ancient papers hidden away in some wealthy family's repository, we, of our generation will probably never know.

Brave blax African sister on French TV, has accumulated overwhelming evidence over the last 20-years against perpetrators in the Rwanda violence in Africa. They are taking one former African army commander to court for his ordering deaths and abetting deaths & furnishing weapons for the slaughter of 800 thousand black Africans of an opposing tribe—the Tutsis.

I just had a sudden memory. Chicago Public Library. Tens of thousands of dusty hardcover books, floors, staircases, of marble inlayed w/turquoise, long reading tables. Stacks, shelves. The mad who sat reading, faces grimacing @ tables trying to keep up the appearance of being sane. –To give themselves a life, of sorts.

It begins—the slow descent into old age; decrepit, degraded—until body gives away utterly, & lets its soul fly free. This body has gotten so accustomed to itself, what a major step into the unknown. Noticed in my 40's slowing down, aches, —but nothing like this failing eye, & painful step of today.

Wednesday, February 5
Was @ Shrink—Jasmin drove me. Talking about how had just sold 4 ebooks last month:

    AT AN EARLY AGE

DOING IT FOR THE MISTRESS
LEADER OF THE PACK
BARS ACROSS HEAVEN

And 1 hardcover book so far this month—JAILHOUSE STUD.

> You are infiltrating the world.
> --Therapist

OM entertained his thoughts as he rushed to Grant Writing Center.

The OM sat on one of his stops—fire hydrant—looked out into cold bleak sky of winter. Saw tenement buildings rising in his scope around him. Glad he was in his right mind & that his thinking had come together when he was 16, 17, which he discovered, sitting in an SRO in Near North Side, Chicago, reading Niche in a old stuffed armchair. Finding: *I can think! What I am reading all makes sense! The sentence fit together into paragraph—showing me an idea!* He thought of Junior lost in the night alleys, curled up in fitful sleep.

PM
It can be difficult caring about someone in trouble—and trying to do something about it.

Junior. Others.

Oh an interesting thing I must say—@ Grant Writing Center, using the free Internet, encountered a client I use to know from a certain establishment, which shall remain nameless (no, not Grace—haven't I tarnished her enough w/scandal?) I asked them, having to be discreet, as we were in a public place:

> Are you still going to *that place* down *there*?

> No not for a long time and I don't intend to go back—not until Ms XX is gone.

> Well Ms XX will never leave, the job's too good, Ms XX will probably still be sitting there long after the agency has shut its doors, hoping it will return.

117

I won't ever go back down there, I'm starting my own place.

So, perhaps the root of some of my troubles there were due to the management—not solely of my own making; but evidently they did not love me enough to try and keep me w/them.

The intelligent officials of the Peoples Republic of China, and nations in Europe are smashing ivory tusks confiscated from wild life poachers—increasingly they are casting down the ivory trade—in order to save the elephant & rhino species & gain world approval instead of world shame!

Thursday, February 6
Seeing that power—the highest, T said: *I give it up to You! Your Way, not mine--I give it up to You.* So maybe I'm only a minor player in the scheme of things.

And not my grandiose dreams of fame…

Am inside Coyote w/coffee seeing vague out of right eye.

Raining outside.

Gather ye rosebuds wile thee may—for time it tis' a passing.

Am glad so much work done. I struggled for it—hope my readers are appreciative of my fine arts; haven't sold but a JS so far this month.

Sit in the window musing thoughts aloud so his lips moved as if talking to himself—which he was.

Oh the Hawk is here w/her wonderful Poodle; sits smiling her poisonous sarcastic grimace on her face—@ a table outside in the rain, because there is no dogs allowed!

Maybe she is outside because she wants to cruise (tho she never partakes).

All parade past—the fallen—most are dopefiends, or alcoholic; one, who I saw nearly die of a drug overdose outside the public library—

face green/grey his body board-stiff as paramedics strapped him onto a stretcher; notice today his hair is graying brown. He is growing old out here—postponing his life, always one drink away from beginning sobriety. Life on hold. Soul on ice. Next the blaxman w/anger he can barely control. Who threw away that plate of food in a rage.

OM considered his life, what he was, what he had become—and he might have to change. Soon he had the small market shopping, & knew what he was going to do when he got home the list of chores so familiar had shrunk—sweep, mop floors—Jasmin done it already—vacuumed & mopped—w/new mop she has purchased; cleaned both bird cages—sheets/pillowcases changed on bed—he was free to work!

Lady of some affluence who had been Lord of her unit—a wonderful apartment w/an amazing view—he saw her march down past the café; he saw them all no one ever had gazed towards the window where he sat, cruising—its because they weren't looking for anything, but just going towards their destination.

The wheels of time are grinding steadily; an internal mechanism is in the cosmos just as if it was physical metal wheels, levers, spokes, gears –that engage in ways you don't understand; it is racing towards a destiny which I have no other control other then what have used superhuman strength to accomplish. *Have faith.*

Again, have faith.

Look @ Theresa of Avila, isn't she one of the most well known in Christendom & beyond? She was denied of self, and worshiped on & on in seclusion—remaining high in the Spirit of God!

No tables, chairs, have been put outside, nor the benches in the parklet—it is drizzling. Exactly one table and one chair outside, that the Hawk had carried out there, —alone, sat.

Spoke w/Singing Man the other day:

119

The lives of a lot of gay men, they have no families—been cast-out—
as they age or sicken they go back to their units; they don't come
out again—they die in there alone.

Which had made him recall similar words coming out of the
transsexual community—about the girls, in particular, who go on the
bottle, or drugs, and start looking so bad, look like men in a dress
once more because their hormones can't work w/the alcohol—and
stop making the effort to beautify themselves—(tweezing, shaving,
plucking, tucking) and they start going downhill and stop taking their
HIV meds, soon you might run into them looking like male hags in
dresses w/ragged stockings & worn-over high heels scrounging in the
free food pantry, but nowhere else, then you don't see them again for
a long time—they retreat back into their rooms and one day you
hear—*oh they found Miss So-And-So, dead in her room. She'd been
dead 3 weeks.*

The caffeine enlivened him—he would have energy to take down his
NOTE-torious JOURNEY Journal notes—but would he have energy to
go home & write?

It is lucky that I can keep on walking.

There was a plan, which gave him energy absolutely, but not w/out
having to monitor his diet. ARRRGH!

God said H/She'd show me a way—to begin painting.

So can't take small Junior home—he's 3 or 4 disasters waiting to
happen & that's when he's on his best behavior.

Time.

Time, said the Lord, *time*. Time for what? My time has come? My
time on earth is done? Time to get a cat? Time for fame?

NOTES are piling up fast now that he was seated indoors @ a desk-
like counter top of Coyote—he would soon exhaust his supply of
paper—he had decided to stay until 3:30—enough time for Junior to
make it here in his time frame—

Pigeons parade regally in the drizzle-wet gutter; stand on their red feet, eyes bright orange—looking for food.

Again substance abuse man goes by in grungy street clothes now his hands on his narrow hips; exasperated, in high agitation; looking around—he's looking for the missing part.

On TV for the first time I've heard of plan that eventually Canada might link up w/USA, just like the EU has united all it's 23 nations.

Antiquated face of the liquor store on that boarded up corner has been peeled off—now the words Tyson's Candy appear—which have waited there, since the 1960's. Yellow age-stained panel under -- work progresses.

> I'm getting' out. I don't mind 'cause I'm getten' out of town.
> --Overheard, street

These are the times of our lives.

In Ho's Dr. Sam called—we went to dine á la Thai food, and conversation.

PM
Even when you are trying to do the right things, this world is very hard. So if you are not always trying to do the right, and are wrong, how impossible it will be for you!

Brick walls apartment falling over—shoved down by heavy-duty earth moving machines. Armchairs abandoned, sit in room w/only 3 walls, no roof; cement dust filters thru the air. Poor peoples housing destroyed for World Cup. —Brazil.

Friday, February 7,
Am now installed in Coyote, lite rain outside; thanks that I have $. Something smells a bit & I hope it ain't me. Today is Friday. Sunday church to look forward to—& the future—for what it might bring; once I have Internet can check my sales regularly—which gives me confidence.

The world has been a history of plunder, war; conquests w/tightening grip only to be relinquished by release of tyrants fist.

A new movie sounds of interest—Monument Men –how Nazis appropriated fine art masterpieces out of nations they conquered; France, Belgium, Austria, Amsterdam, Poland, SS Generals shipping wooden crates of priceless art treasures back by railroad to their chalets & mansions in Germany & the allies got it back aided by courageous Rose Valland (Rose Valland Saves The Paintings of France, From Nazis. Acrylic on Canvas; 20″ X 24″). She was a curator in the Louve, Paris's most famous museum, —thanks to her meticulous records the Allies were able to trace where the Nazi scum had shipped their stolen goods—traced back to make returns.

The Singing Man comes by, talks about the Human condition. People are not happy until they make a change in their lives—then they still not happy.

A scene of interest occurs; 3 blax gangster type men enter the café—low down types; one whose fit of rage I'd mentioned several months back; they sat, then got up and kept moving around. Was speaking w/Malaysian on the phone @ the time, when the men came in and began loud-talking: *what's all that!* She demanded to know, @ which point I just said: *I'll talk to you later*, and calmly PU my gear and moved over to the other side of the café.

Jasmin to come over to do her cleaning & help install me on Internet; she must use her giant brain to figure it out! I can't/won't.

Today is a blue day.

It is good when human beings help PU another human being who lays fallen & this is exactly what City Services has done for XX when he had gone indoors in pain, sickness, & most likely depression; retreated into his unit & unplugged the phone.

Humans do this, some of us, like an ailing animal goes off deep into the forest alone to die.

Singing Man & Gary & others including myself were concerned. Adult Protective Services was called & they gained access to his unit & he talked to them; they promptly set up all these services—a home help support, MOW, ect, also for Communist John from church—they have sent a lady to clean his unit several times a week & go shopping for him. As the Malaysian says: *He is living high on the hog under capitalism yet claims he's a Communist.* –OH, tho sick & not eating himself, XX had plenty of C-food in stock and his cat was fine.

You're jumpy. Prison jumpy.

Dr Sam talks about upon transition, many new men are being placed into a world they have had positively no training for—not prepared for—some grow up only partially in the world of boys & other not @ all depending on acceptance by other natural-born males. Some T-girls grew up surrounded by sisters & female classmates who took them in—making easier for them to adapt their ways to those of women.

Life pounds on like a heartbeat—w/beautiful music.

OM decided not to go by empty Ho's benches in rain, but to go home & be glad he had a home to go to.

He hoped he would be able to dwell in his humble abode & ignite his fine arts career; as well as to continue to affix most of his typewritten novels & books into digital so as to preserve, enable world-wide distribution.

To win the race—to gain the Great Prize of Life.

> I kept myself alive so I am here for you now.
> --TM, upon wining the Great Prize

Tomorrow is another day—so we try again.

Be proud of yourself Red Jordan.

Put a lock on it. Let me explain the following thread. You have dedicated yourself to God; (The Eternal) means first/foremost complete obedience. You make your pledge to God, but soon break it—because the flesh is all too weak. But by telling God to put a lock on your pledge, you give permission for God to intervene in your state of disobedience. To tap you on the shoulder (which can be quite a heavy event) to draw your attention back to your state of miss-alignment.

PM
Baz on wei over!

> Boring is as boring does.
> --Young Man Baz

Coffeyed & discussed for several hours w/Baz. We considered living here, where to live in future, me telling him how so many of us are so uncertain where we might be living in a year from now—if the city continues its move-outs, and escalation of spectacular greed.

Yes, this place has become a city of spectacular greed.

Brother Baz said:

> I'm driving these yups around; they get in my car, they're all engaged in themselves. I hear them talk, all white men, all tekkies—they have no idea, they have no clue.

The young man's tan fingers tapped down the table-top where it ended & fell away into empty space. *The edge.* He said. *We are all walking the edge, here in this city of San Francisco.*

2 Egyptian former presidents are now on trial in Egypt which is a mass of protests & fire! Men in 3 piece suits hurl bricks @ government building side by side w/men in Islamic robes throwing paving stones; an old woman in black burka sits on top shoulders of a wave protesters w/poster of one of the corrupt tyrants which she rips in half and thrust the pieces into the air victoriously! —All trying to bring down their corrupt government! --TV

Saturday, February 8
Ancient footprints 1 million years old found! A family of 5-humans. Distinctly 2 children, 1 an adult male; very clear!

Am in Coyote—raining out. Inside w/coffee.

Am seriously focusing on weight loss. MOW has salt. That must be partially the problem. Will rinse food! Yes!

See someone dreamed up idea of giving homeless meth-addicted people a low cost Internet. —As long as I have mine, its fine! Imagine a society where a poor OM, senior w/their own business can't see his sales results, or build his books except @ public library w/its 1-hour limit; this pathetic KKKapitalism devouring the globe.

Wear & tear on the human body—wear & tear on the human spirit. —What is worse?

A whole table of tekkie-yups sits behind me; they are white, they are mostly young—the best & brightest of the human race— they are all engaged in insider professional work:

Teach them compassion. Says the Lord.

> I'm in the system— ABC, CBS (major TV channels). I get a salary, bonuses; that's why its good for me. I wrote a copy for CBS.

<u>ME.</u>

> Do I want to sell their products? That's the question.

> I'm getting into real-estate right now.

One of them walks by, middle age creepy appearance; geek; his expression as mentally twisted as a homeless person, but well groomed & men's expensive casual clothes. But the lines in his face reflect growing discontent by now because of his human failure.

2-men in street, apart, insular, both stomping. –Each for separate reasons. –They are all the way crazy.

Oh, the tip jar was robbed again—Asian man. Puts his hand into it & runs off.

> Its like a game to them. We have them on surveillance. They PU them, lock them up, their right back out. They aren't being prosecuted.

Two incidents happened on his way home. Crossing the entrance to the Ho's a white bitch yuppie young female in a nice new car pulled across the driveway —completely blocking the pedestrian sidewalk; sitting there selfishly waiting for a parking place to open up. –Had she pulled up only one or two more feet it would have allowed the OM to cross w/his cane.

ARE YOU GOING TO MOVE? He bellowed @ the foolish bitch. Bent down to glare @ her thru the window a moment. He bellowed this 4 or 5 times — ARE YOU GOING TO MOVE! while walking out of his way in front of her car and back to the sidewalk continuing on, and bellowed it again @ her window, in which she sat stony face, lips pursed, white face glaring on thru her windshield not moving nor acknowledging one fucken' thing.

Of course the sensitive OM did not feel good about having to do this bellowing either. Frankly he felt very worn down by this engulfment of rude, selfish yuppies that don't have a clue and too rich too.

War is never pleasant.

Then in the shop where he buys sparkling water occasionally, a white young man stood there @ the counter and rudely the OM stomped up, interrupted shopkeeper asking to tell the other employee to go get his Sparkling Water for him, as he was carrying so much stuff he didn't want to knock anything off the shelves of the small cramped aisles; and the rich white yuppie turned & gave the OM a strange look— afraid I'm a crazy homeless who will pull a gun on him? & shoot him dead.   And he's looking @ me sharply and I kept apologizing *I'm sorry sir, I'm sorry,* realizing how rude he'd been to interrupt the man's transaction— (OM had been so rude because he was still highly upset & agitated.) And here is this privileged man, staring down @ him; handsome—a perfect specimen.

Just hope our children—among the poor—will keep up the fight.

PM

Feel so old, so tired. I don't see many people like me out in the streets any more—no old, no poor, we engulfed in a tidal wave of rich, upscale well dressed, in-a-hurry yups; feel like my dark skin black friends, who walk thru SF and see no other blax faces—and have long since departed:

> What I like about Oaktown, cross over the bridge and I see black/brown faces—but not here in SF anymore.
> --Upscale black government worker, TM

> It's a shame what they've done to SF, a shame. And nobody says anything!
> --Older blax gentleman, poor, on Diviz bus

> *Consider the lilies of the field—they do not toil, nor do they spin, but look how beautifully they are arrayed.*
> --Old Testament, Holy Bible

I feel like crying, but I can't—T. All because of this stupid class-warfare.

I really feel surrounded by this madness, and afraid.

One thing is so true—after every boom there's a bust. If the bust is far & deep enough, coinciding w/some other kind of change, geographical, economic, etcetera, it will end this forced occupation by the selfish rich—maybe drastically.

> A global shift of economics
> An earthquake
> A new application that all the yuppies must flock to that new epicenter—maybe Canada where the quantum super computer is being developed:

Quantum Super Computer; the working mechanism has to be processed @ 460 degrees below zero Fahrenheit—which is a few degrees above absolute zero— at this level, the different X's and O's begin to float around together, one now free to superimpose itself upon the other and the other on it—both continuing to work simultaneously, and independently of each other, thus creating a new information stream which works a million times faster then the already fast silicon chip process—it will revolutionize the world.

So am afraid of this vast army of the wealthy. But God can turn the tables on them!

He felt better after seeing all the violence & hell on TV going on all over the world.

> She's a switch hitter.
>
> A switch hitter on the regular side or the funny side?
>
> She likes 'em both. The funny side more; she likes broads more. — Femmes.
> --LUCKY & MICKEY

You know, life really shouldn't be as difficult as it is. One says she only stays alive because of her finches & fish. Another lives to caretake his cats. I have my parrots. The lucky ones have a companion, maybe even children.

Sunday, February 9,
And forgive us our trespasses as we forgive those who trespass against us.

Realize by now long ago he'd forgiven the hideous Hawk—by extensive process of wearing away stony hearts on the long shuffling march up to the communion table—& partaking the Body & Blood; back & forth over & over for weeks, months, years.

He had many prayers to put up, when he could be more centered in himself, alone, in privacy.

They had throughally discussed the Dean:

> Are they legally married or is it just a domestic partnership—the old fashion gay marriage?

128

Are they butch & femme?
Dean make-overs.

In the front of the cathedral tonight's chorale angelically sung the Lord(ess) Prayer: *For thine is the kingdom & the power & the glory...* which as we know Jesus did not say @ all, but was lines which were only added 1,000 years later.

Information; says the Lord, —like a breath of life.

The Church needs to be modernized.

Salt was used for soldiers pay. Solarium. Soldiers paid in salt— which gave rise to the word salary.

300AD to 600AD; half the revenue of China was in salt.

Priest Jude delivered a fascinating sermon, concerning *you are the salt of the earth.*

Disgruntled, can't get into the inner circle around the communion table. The OM sat back away from it—on an actual *chair*, glowering.

PM
Stone tracery. These are the strips of stone between the beautiful stained glass windows colored blue, red, yellow, green, purple.

Monday, February 10
Am @ Coyote after a wild insane crazed morning; knocking, door banging, barking, and parrots screeching.

> 10AM Roach Man
> 10:15 Jasmin & Henry (dog)
> 12:30 MOW

> When you go out in this town you don't get dressed up to go out— you don't get dressed in a suit.
> --Young male Yuppie

The air was polluted by a smoker; so he moved further away.

Jasmin hooked up my Internet.

The sun bored a hole in the sky—far distant & dim—thru the day fog.

Plaintive reggae music marked time, beat pacing beat; accompanied by an edgy voice Jamaican singer.

The sun had gone out. Suddenly it grew cold. *My ears are cold—* OM decided to leave for the Ho's where the sun would still be—it had slid along down the line of building tops towards its planetary destination—the other side of the world, disappearing beyond us.

He was a little sad, having talked to no one.

Suddenly he was not alone; as Jasmin was around –much more often.

The sun poked out golden—the page he was writing turned bright in this new-found sun.

The whole day turns bright.

God hid Red tucked away in a little corner of Coyote, outside, along its frontage under eves where pigeons roost.

White lady drug hustler walks by purposeful stride speaking into cell phone: *I'm coming by there to get it, I'm almost there now! Don't make this anymore difficult then it has to be!* –No doubt extracting money or dope from some hapless customer.

The conditions seemed OK, the Malaysian was there, agreeable to the effort; he had come prepared w/his scissors & breadcrumbs. The bound-foot pigeon flew down and was eating. But tho he tried was unable to catch it.

He'd bend down stiffly on his arthritic body and grasp for the bird, who'd fluttered its wings batting its wings against his legs & hobbled off quickly and remained just out of reach.

He was sad because of this.

The day had gone pale white, cold, sunless; the pigeon, w/others, flapped its way on strong wings off the scene in a direct beeline somewhere to the tenement roofs further downtown—to be w/its flock, in a home, warm.

PM
Internet not finished being hooked up.

They struggle onward; they live in sin not knowing. Their day soon passed. --*You are to give rise to something that is to come.*

Tuesday, February 11
A church may be devoured by devils—it is written—that Satan will seize the highest posts of human achievement, to give him more rule over human kind—which he hates. So the logical place to conquer would be high powers & principalities such as the government, the clergy, not to mention heads of businesses, corporations etc, so that not only the rank and file of humanity reflects 1 out of 3 of us being a devil out to corrupt the rest—but it extends from the lowest position on up—however my point is, that to turn your back on the church because of its apparent dirty double-dealings—as I did w/that first church long ago in my childhood, and the 2nd, the gay church, — saying: *it is a corrupt place, there is no God(ess) there,* would be a mistake; humanity flocks to its shuls, mosques, churches, and other places of worship—these people are full of need, pain, hope, and faith! Thus it is their tremendous faith in the Divine alone, which justifies the existence of this human institution; it is their faith in the Divine which elevates this religious institution far above its accountable human achievement; it is their faith in the Eternal which raises an average simple religious household of 1, 2, 3, or 4 persons —in a collective way—of the necessity of a mass of human souls thronging there w/their belief in God, their courtship of God, which accelerates their prayers still further! Their prayers cast up like sweet incense!

So join the throng—worship en mass, there is power in that!

You are well protected—by rings within rings.

Well—am @ Coyote—sun is here.

131

Just as he arrived the 2 blax street sweeper employees came & sat right by the entrance—which is the best place to be as the effects of drifts of cigarette smoke usually go up the block from that point. TM sat immediately @ the opposite end.

The day before, an Asian lass had seated herself there, right by the door—and her chain smoking smoke blew along the entire frontage of Coyote. Usually the wind did blow up Polk from down in the TL—in the direction of Upper Polk ritzy area.

The insane man who is young who is such a crazed, mean, demented fool passed by, but did not act out. Often he is disappeared. No doubt arrest by police & jailed—for violent aggravated trouble.

—This weather is like autumn would be in a more Eastern City— wind blows. Sweat dripped down under his great green coat.

No Gary will be there—as had seen him elsewhere, sitting in his car.

Hence, again he sat—outermost fringe of Coyote frontage—in a corner—alone!

Not alone Red Jordan—

So maybe this why God has me seated alone, to better talk w/me. To take these NOTES of an observer that one does not take when engaged in merry conversation.

So the OM sat there in the sun in the corner—entertaining himself inside his head w/fantasies of fame. Fame for a purpose.

Learned a new word yesterday from church brother Denis— Greenwashing. As when corporations mislead the public pretending to be Green—environmentally friendly— when they are not! Like whitewashing. To whitewash the ugly truth w/a misleading clean orderly veneer.

It had been bothering his soul—the plight of the bound foot pigeon, so as the OM climbed uphill towards the Ho's, he prayed feverently from his soul—for release of the creature.

132

Then a miracle happened!

Not sure if I witnessed a miracle today or not… but the bound-foot pigeon came to us quickly today—even after the bright direct sun had gone, cold grey; it flew to us—Mark was there, limber, tho older, he was able to get down on his knees—and he was able to capture it! And, as he held up the pigeon and I poked under its fur-like grey stomach feathers revealing its gnarled filthy red feet —saw—the binding had already been released! I took my scissors and cut away the excess string, then off he/she flew!

Every time I'd seen this pigeon for a month (see JOURNEY journals) the wire or string had remained firmly in place! Hobbling the pigeon who must jump & hop to move.

Freed pigeon! And the Lord(ess) told me: *you will free many.*

PM

> That summer of 1959, especially that summer—before their lives fell into disrepair. They looked so good up there. A bottle of beer they shared; the admiration of their crowd; & at home Mickey giving it to Lucy hot & hard, and the femme was accepting. Opening her arms & spreading her thighs in wanting, everynight.
>
> They looked so good that a woman bought them both drinks—she was a supervisor at a plant and made $25,000 a year and had to put on a skirt to get it. Mickey held up her glass in acknowledgement in the smoky bar.
> --LUCY & MICKEY

New Internet still don't work.

Assassin of Martin Luther King says he acted alone—but he acted in concert w/the times—of white southern bigots, pro-slavery racists in Memphis who were everywhere from the common citizen to local police departments, to high government officials.

Syrian children are talking about difference between bombs, and rockets, or tank shells—in this picture we see the children have some of these deadly bombs lined up in the dirt, like toys—which they have found.

280-Syrian civilians being murdered every day.

Wednesday, February 12
Internet connected! Saw Amazon ebook sales!

The street—here they pass from every walk of life; one born deranged, crazy, walking, hauls a messy bundle of used clothes & miscellaneous recyclables in a broke cart; one born average, walking in a hurry, who possesses paycheck, checking account, rental agreements.

Flutes & bells accompany this pageant of the streets, emitted from the café's speakers.

Well the day has been madcap—now finally @ Coyote—just called jail to see if Junior is in sheriff's custody.

Mailed off Bancroft shipment.

PM

> Alexander! Mr. Lee's voice was perpetually excited, as if he was always on the edge of hysteria, but at the mention of the name Alexander D'Oro, the middle aged man fairly flew into a fit: THAT SHOE LESS BLACK SISSY WITH NO SOX! I KNOW ALEXANDER! HOW COULD I FORGET!
> --@ Mr. Lee's--STREET OF DREAMS

Thursday, February 13
Am @ Coyote. No one here. Singing Man just leaving.

Pleasant hot sun weight already down a tad & planning to eat @ reception tonite.

The OM sat in his brown trousers & checked black/grey (Goodwill) shirt, donated tie from Dan; great green coat from Jasmin, & blue baseball cap, (found); sat, feet in construction boots (Jasmin bought) firmly planted, legs spread; in a better world someone would appear, go kneel before him and proceed to lick/suck OM's private parts—as do our own ancient ancestor monkey tribe, the Bonobos.

Monkey tribe—which has sex w/each other all day long.

Well I was obedient to the *calling* in my heart—so here I sit in this place, SF. I hatched out my master works of writing & a number of Fine Art's paintings here.

2 Hawks—the Teeter-Winged Hawks, appear; the Teeter-Winged Hawks don't flap their wings any more then necessary, just to attain altitude, then they sit, floating on air, teetering back & forth, up/down to catch the constant currents. It is a mated pair. Wide wing-spread hover in air way above human thongs in the grey blue air, hunting pray—other birds. This is why the flock of pigeons flew off just moments ago.

He sat on fire hydrant; it vibrated under his ass—on wei to Grace—Hoopla.

200 Reader volunteers @ church that Jeffrey must coordinate! People often ask: *I really like the way you read, why don't you read more often?* They don't realize how many other people also want to do the job!

Our church is/is not a historical monument. Debate rages on as to when Grace was actually founded. —Because the church founded first in 1886—burned down in 1906 in the Great San Francisco fire—then rebuilt again where she is today— had her first asp built up to the transepts where the Cross meets and including part of the church w/some pews & the crypt; then the campanile a distance apart, and the completed structure wasn't until 1940's—so this particular edition of the church isn't 100 years old.

Interesting conversation before the proceedings began—w/senior woman, about our president Obama, boycotting the Russian Olympic games in Sochi:

> Well they are boycotting the Olympics because of Putan's stance on cutting GLBT rights.

No it wasn't. They're boycotting because of something else, not the gay, no.

You mean them harboring Edward Snowdon, who released all those National Secrets?

Yes, maybe that was it.

No, I distinctly heard all over the media that president Obama would boycott the games in Russia and also Angela Merkal would boycott them from Germany; that is a royal snub when the heads of nations don't go to your Olympiad!

Anyway this woman insisted over and over that gay support wasn't the reason—straight people who are challenged by us are so resistant to attributing to us the slightest power.

Maybe she didn't know this was to be a GLBT Marriage Equality *celebration!* First a lesbian choir sang, then a men's gay choir from Oakland.

It was a wonderful service celebrating GLBT marriage rights.

Never would have dreamed this in my youth of 15, 16, in 1957; in '58, in the streets; in those forbidden gay clubs owned by mafia gangsters, that scene of red light from police cars & Paddy wagons flashing across building walls; rolling up every where we tried to assemble.

Such sopranos! The dikes clear high voices, so beautiful. They sing of their love for another women. Now the gay men's choir—of beautiful baritone tones, deep-voiced reverberation out of manly chests. LGBTQ. Revelations—my gay community! Our logos is now used all over this earth!

Gay Men's choir sang the powerful Negro Spiritual Go Down Moses—*way down to Egypt land—tell ole pharaoh, to let My People Go!*

Many T's are so unaware—so anti-social. A T gal caused quite a commotion down @ the end of my aisle; fidgeting w/all her things, then finally running away, out of the service, —right across the front of the stage—then out the Cathedral's sturdy mahogany doors. – Maybe she thought it was her in particular who was being celebrated!

As God would have, so here we sit—in a row; one beside another; TG—(MTF), L, TG –(FTM), L, G, G.

God starts first informing the intellectual mind—plays on our reason—then touches our hearts, our spiritual soul.

He saw his works, he gave each one to God—they were like a flock of birds; they were going on the way he'd tried to send them & not getting very far but suddenly all changed up direction and now winged their way to where God had a purpose for them.

Flying towards God instead of towards his own desires; flying towards destiny.

Shield the joyous. That saying is part of an ancient prayer. How important this is; how many times as an unbeliever living in the flesh—and in ideas of his own mind's concoction— he'd been having an uproarious fun time, people partying, reveling, then hell would break out, some soul among them holding up a butcher knife gripped in both hands, eyes wild, annunciated by strobe lights flicking murderous jealous rage against the barroom walls.

The round full moon pale, luminous—lit and surrounded by white clouds set deep in night sky floated on a sea of ink jet black.

PM
Nada. –Yet much transpired this day—racing around.

Friday, February 14
When I tell people how old I am, I'm actually bragging.

Madcap day w/Jasmin PU me, complete w/small dog—Henry— & drop off my laundry sacks, then on to Castro Mission clinic drop off paper for parking permit, home health care attendant for Jasmin's car—then on to eye doctor @ The General.

137

In the waiting room there is a subtext among the ordinary people, of those of us who are not ordinary. The doctors, myself, another artist—sexual art photographer Mark C. Have run into him here. We are getting older, we have eye problems. We both need our eyes to do our work!

PM
Nada.

Is my calling to be like Denis—to make my life the church—attending for 50 years?

Saturday, February 15
Am @ Coyote. Me tired—weight problem. Yesterday didn't walk @ all—Jasmin drove me to 2 appointments & also straight home. Baz PU me for coffee. Just walked 2.5 blocks—1 of them uphill.

Weight up. Today have walked ½ of my route—limit to 2 MOW per day (discarding rice, canned fruit, bread, potatoes) but unlimited hamburger meat patties (cooked by Jasmin) w/tomato paste & olive oil—from now on will limit to 1 big patty w/trimmings, only.

So the trannys are always left alone—the gay men flurry on— in tuxedos, off to the ball arm in arm w/each other—the dikes the same, in plaid flannel shirts, trousers & boots scurry off w/their dike partners to set up housekeeping—so unless you got a T-boy friend, or a T community you might spend the rest of your life alone.

The OM sat there—he was thinking about space travel—about habitable worlds, about home for migrating to on other planets—he thought he might finish his mighty Sci-Fi series; he mulled over scripts of fantasies in his brain—

Looked forward to accessing the Internet that night if possible.

He had once counted his small collection of friends on his hands as collateral—but now they had spread themselves further away across the geography of America—& some he barely saw 4 times per year, 1 not @ all, another constantly questioning moving out of state plus had already moved 45 minute drive away—Jasmin lived @ the opposite

138

end of SF, near to the border of another town; none of them liked the changes going on in this corrupted city & want to get away. Some simply won't be able to survive if their units are bought up & they are forced out.

Oh, I guess Junior is gone for good—no one on the block has seen him & he's not in jail. Liza (Lady w/Dog #1) saw him 3 weeks ago, and said he looked bad—but no more sightings since.

The sky looks like it is full of rain & a few drops have squeezed out.

It is time to depart—go to Ho's.

> Kilobyte is 1,000 bytes
> Megabyte is 1,000,000
> Gigabyte is 1,000,000,000
> Terabyte is 1,000,000,000,000

Denis knows stuff.

Will one of these gigantic-memory computers be the application which drives all these infernal tekkies back out of town from where they came? The advancement which makes tens of thousands of them obsolete w/a single keystroke?

PM
Nada.

Sunday, February 16
Calf-Jasmin over, vacuumed, mopped all floors, & is cleaning kitchen. When she came in the Animal Control Department was outside the building—they came in and confiscated cat from unit downstairs—the person is in the hospital. Cat removed for 14 days—its fate remaining to be seen. Will it be put up for adoption, or returned to owner:

> My gawd it was terrifying! Jasmin sights the Animal Control
> outside, and the parrots begin a fearsome SQUAWKING!
> Screeching at the top of their lungs, I yell—*Jasmin! Cover up the birds*
> *quick! Shut them up before the Animal Control hears them!*
> --Red, raconteeering

139

Jasmin cleaning refrigerator and making horrible sounds of disgust:

Oh God! Mold growing in your coffee cup!

OM very upset @ computer, which Jasmin had changed his settings—for in the stress of it he saw how angry he was w/his life—his disappointments; he sat 1/2 way up the hill on a fire hydrant.

How good to be in the house of the Lord/ess.

They are singing Alleluia!

They were playing beautiful music. We, the assembled congregation are singing: *we are marching in the light of God*—but the trained singers were singing it in an African language.

We can do it. See w/life—not w/anger & hate. We can do it! --Only thru the help of Jesus Christ, if you are as messed up as me.

PM
I must say it is a bit difficult for me to have Jasmin so close—and in my house again, —as she was for 16 ½ years. Plays on my emotions.

House is very clean—she has done an excellent job!

Monday, February 17
Be strong Red Jordan—because you are strong.

@ Coyote—sun beginning to shine hot—No OGM—they evidently have been another place—I myself will stay here—no one is here but the hideous one & now another of us comes, sits down—all else is vacant out here have we T's nothing other to do?

One thing about T —appearances has it—a line of 3 of us some 15-feet apart—one Old Man, 2 women, each @ their own table/chair. But when the 2 women speak, oddly to the casual passerby, it is male voices that come out of their throats; they are sadly confined to their male range. Well, as I said—apparently we have nothing better to do...

140

No more Olde Jolly. No more Junior. No more anybody.

The Singing Man came by later, told me he had a Junior sighting, days ago—on Polk Strassa—but way way up, around Broadway.

The Hawk trots down the street—rather, giant poodle drags her— which is the only drag the bitch will do—surely she notices the 3 of us TS are the only ones out here—yet we are divided. —C'est la vie.

The human race is 80% water, malleable, changeable, adaptable.

This world is severe—it is fierce.

We spoke of STEPS before.

I see—looking back—many steps—the Lord/ess takes me thru in discovering the mind of God pour moi, vs. my own mind—& things have changed. I stand here on the road—already having passed the crossroads quite a while back; of decision-making, & still await my true purpose, calling, job, yoke, —for the remainder of my short days on this mortal earth.

Talked w/young coffee server about a hideous book review she received from a critic—it is one who advertises themselves as a reader for an unknown writer's book who will either give the author a free review—if they feel like it, or a paid-for review. She paid a small amount of cash—and received in return a low, horrible review, and one which reflected that this critic had not truly read her book. We tossed about the idea of exchanging the favor of writing a review for each other…

Climb to the stars Red Jordan!

> They made it to age 80, that's very good, then you get sick from all kinds of things, first one thing then another; well we all have to die of something.
> --The Malaysian

Ah! The ex-bound foot bird appears! S/he wing flaps against my arm to draw my attention—

The OM had absolutely no crumbs in his great green coat pocket—but the clever Malaysian spied a food box sitting on top of one of those Homeland Security garbage cans, which are impossible to access—so that mostly people have to set their garbage ontop of it or beside it. OM shuffled over and found a bread rind in a box, and some fragmented food-like scrambled eggs—perfect nourishment for a bird!

He brought it back, hand placing each morsel on the railing for the bird, which it pecked up, and finally shook out the remainder onto the cement right under the bench where he left it to dine. Industriously pecking, its fat feathered stomach resting against the cement, its head bobbing up/down, up/down, up/down and bright bead orange eyes glistening as it scavenging each morsel.

The pigeon looked much better—so much so he hardly had recognized it! Walking on both feet, not hobbling nearly as much & getting around! It was freed!

It is much better—now it dined.

Oh—turns out the lady argued w/over GLBTQ issue @ Grace is a very sympathetic to us, she just was arguing about the matter-- *because she likes to argue!* That's all! —That's her only reason! Which is a good thing—to resist the evil machine. She is supportive to all human rights—and has a very liberated mind. Thus says the Malaysian, who is her friend.

PM
Am glad in every way shape form for Jasmin cleaning my house! This home health service of the State government is certainly a great benefit to me!

There has been so many deaths. Big, milestone deaths. Worst, & 1st, the living death of my mom—to mental illness. 2nd, my beloved dad died. Then, Jasmin left me, an ongoing separation pain. This pressed on a background of heartache; all the little deaths of various loved animals on the way.

All await in heaven.

What happens when you penetrate in to the hidden jungles, the inner-most remote places—you still just find other people—like yourself—other human beings, other human thoughts. No matter how esoteric, they are only human thoughts.

Seek My Ways.

--God has given me these words!

Red Jordan Arobateau
Wednesday, February 26, 2014
12:30 AM, Pacific Standard
 Time
San Francisco, CA

www.ingramcontent.com/pod-product-compliance
Lightning Source LLC
Chambersburg PA
CBHW051413280526
45785CB00003B/1053